THE MIDDLE-WAY MEDITATION INSTRUCTIONS

The Middle-way Meditation Instructions:
Developing Compassion through Wisdom

Based on Mipham Rinpoche's
Gateway to Knowledge (Tib. *mkhs 'jug*)

by

Khenchen Thrangu, Rinpoche
Geshe Lharampa

Translated by
Ken and Katia Holmes

The Namo Buddha Seminar
1390 Kalmia Avenue
Boulder, CO 80304-1813 USA
Telephone: (303) 449-6608
E-mail: cjohnson@ix.netcom.com
Rinpoche's web site: www.rinpoche.com

Acknowledgments

We would like to thank Tomiko Yabumoto for the immense work of transcribing this text from the original tapes. We would also like to thank Jean Johnson and Terry Lukas, for editing it. Thanks to Demetrius for the cover design. The front and back photographs were taken by Clark Johnson outside Taos, New Mexico. We would also like to especially thank Michele Papen Daniel for making this book possible.

Note

Technical words are italicized the first time that they are used to alert the reader that they may be found in the Glossary.

Tibetan words are given as they are pronounced, not spelled in Tibetan. For their actual spelling, see the Glossary of Tibetan Terms.

We also follow the convention of using B.C.E. (Before Common Era) for B. C. and C.E. (Common Era) for A. D.

These teachings were given at Samye Ling Monastery in Scotland in June of 1981.

ISBN 0-9628026-6-2

Table of Contents

Lhagtong (Vipashyana) by Thrangu Rinpoche

Foreword

Two and a half millennia ago the Buddha graced our earth and taught a remarkable set of philosophical proposals. He proposed, to greatly simplify, that all our happiness and all of our suffering and the multitude of our problems in this life are due to one thing: conceptual mind. By the endless pursuit of happiness, through obtaining more material goods, and the continual desire for honor and gain, we experience disappointment. This condition is very poignant these days, because we live in a society that is awash with material goods. We are constantly bombarded by messages to buy in order to be happier, yet our happiness is not any greater than that of the peasants of impoverished India 2,000 years ago. The Buddha taught that the path to happiness lies in examining the mind.

This examination happens in meditation. We begin this practice on the Buddhist path by developing tranquillity through stable meditation. This practice involves a process of "taming the mind." The meditator focuses mindfulness on an object such as the breath. When distractions in the form of thoughts arise, we simply keep refocusing on the object. The beginning of this process is likened to the raging torrent of a mountain stream. The meditator is overwhelmed by the strength and constant occurrence of thoughts manufactured by the mind. But gradually, by meditating again and again and applying the instructions of mindfulness, the mind begins to calm, and the meditator finds that an object is no longer necessary. Rather, with experience, the mind remains focused and stable. At this point the mind becomes tranquil and peaceful. This stage of meditation is likened to a slow, meandering river. The final stage of shamatha meditation is described as a vast ocean with only gentle waves. This process has been described in greater detail in Thrangu Rinpoche's *A Guide to Shamatha Meditation*.

After the meditator finds that the mind can be placed without distraction, the meditator then begins to examine what creates this external phenomena of these appearances and feelings. When we examine these thoughts and feelings, we find that they have no substantial reality and are said the be "empty." Seeing the transitory nature and insubstantiality of mind's activity is seeing the emptiness. While teachings on emptiness are found in numerous teachings of the Buddha, it was Nagarjuna who systematized these teachings into the Middle-way (Skt. Madhyamaka) school. The Madhyamaka school is part of the mahayana movement of Buddhism which migrated to China, Tibet, Korea and other far eastern countries.

Because emptiness is a concept difficult to grasp, there have been many attempts to find a better word, but *shunyata* in Sanskrit and *tong pa nyid* in Tibetan both refer to the word empty as say a glass being "empty" of water when there is no water left in it. This emptiness can be demonstrated for qualities such as tall-short, beautiful-ugly, smart-dumb, good-bad. These qualities are empty because they rely entirely on the context of the situation, as our mind perceives it, not on any inherent, actual characteristic of the object. These qualities are shown to be relative and therefore empty of concrete existence.

We may now say something like, "Well, emptiness applies to qualities, but it cannot apply to real, solid objects." Thrangu Rinpoche then often raises his hand and says, "Look at this. I think it is a hand, you think it is a hand, a hundred people would say it is a hand." But is it really, inherently a hand or is "hand" another concept that our mind attributes to this thing? Then Rinpoche goes through classical Madhyamaka logic, saying, "No, this isn't a hand, it is fingers; no, it isn't a hand because it has bones; no, it isn't a hand because it is flesh" and so on, showing that it is actually our mind that has created the concept of a "hand." When we examine it carefully, we find that there is nothing but an idea put together of components. This may seem obvious, but what has been logically demonstrated is that what we see as a solid, external object is actually also empty; it is not inherently a hand, but rather these components are in a particular arrangement or context and ascribed by our mind as one solid thing.

This idea that mind creates our universe as we experience it is not limited to some philosophers who lived 2,000 years ago. In our century, modern physicists have demonstrated the emptiness of external objects by showing what we see as a hand is actually a huge collection of moving atoms that don't resemble anything like a hand.

A "hand" is actually made of carbon, hydrogen, and oxygen atoms which are vibrating forms of energy wave-particles that are flying off into space in large numbers. The only reason we call it a "hand" is that our mind "sees" a particular organization of atoms as "a hand." In fact, these atoms are over 99% empty space and are not solid by any means.

We may then ask why is all this demonstration of emptiness important? Rinpoche usually answers with the example of Milarepa, who was able to completely master the emptiness of phenomena. After he had done so, Milarepa was able to do such things as pass his hand right through "solid" rocks. But more relevant to us is that for us to be able to reach enlightenment, the end of all suffering, we must completely understand our mind and how this mind of ours actually creates the phenomenal world that we experience.

In this series of lectures on *The Middle-way Meditation Instructions* the great practitioner and scholar Mipham Rinpoche gives an extensive explanation of how to meditate on the mahayana path as it came to Tibet through the great Indian practitioner Kamalashila. While shamatha and vipashyana and the impeccable behavior of following the Vinaya are essential on the path, one needs to cultivate three more qualities: compassion, bodhichitta, and prajna to achieve enlightenment. Having compassion for others is a central concept in Buddhism because if we think only of ourselves, we will never develop the necessary motivation for achieving enlightenment. Bodhichitta is an expansion of this compassion to every sentient being including all animals, beings in other realms, all races, and excluding no one.

Finally, we cannot help others unless we do this intelligently and skillfully and so we must develop true wisdom in order to help others. To help in this vast enterprise the Middle-way includes special techniques beyond shamatha and vipashyana meditation for how to work with the mind and what to do when obstacles arise in meditation. These are all given in this text in great detail, along with a discussion about meditation on the vajrayana path. One may wonder why the vajrayana was included in this text. The answer is that in Tibet, the meditation of the hinayana, of the mahayana and particularly the Middle-way path, and the vajrayana were all practiced together. All three forms of meditation were studied and practiced, since together they are the complete path.

We are indeed fortunate to have Thrangu Rinpoche give the commentary on this text which unfortunately has not yet been translated into English. The Thrangu Tulku and Mipham Rinpoche had a close connection in their previous lives. Thrangu Rinpoche with his vast experience of teaching the dharma to Westerners over the last twenty years has always felt that the Middle-way is important for Westerners to understand and here in this exposition he is able to explain the meditation that goes along with these teachings.

The Middle-way instructions teach us how to practice on and off the meditation cushion. It teaches us how the path to achieve liberation is an extension of our meditation experience into the activity of our daily lives.

Clark Johnson, Ph. D.

Chapter 1

How the Middle-way Was Introduced into Tibet

The reason for practicing *Dharma* is to develop an understanding of the actual nature of phenomena. To fully understand the true nature of phenomena[1], one has to practice meditation. There are many different methods of meditation to attain this realization. We can first meditate on the emptiness (Skt. *shunyata*) aspect of the nature of phenomena. This was expounded by the Buddha when he gave teachings in what is called the second turning of the wheel of Dharma[2] These teachings concern the emptiness of external phenomena such as trees and rocks. After the passing away of the Buddha, these teachings of the second turning were further elaborated by great teachers or mahasiddhas such as Nagarjuna who helped found the *Middle-way* (Skt. *Madhyamaka*) school. These great masters presented logical arguments to prove the validity of the teachings on emptiness. For instance, the Buddha stated the emptiness of phenomena in the *Heart* sutra by saying, "There is no form, there is no sound, there is no smell, there is no taste," and so on. Nagarjuna and other great teachers presented logical arguments for proving things are empty. By studying these arguments intellectually, students can develop an understanding of emptiness and can then develop confidence in the fact that phenomena are indeed empty[3].

The Story of Kamalashila

The theory of the emptiness of phenomena was the basis of the teaching and practice known as the Middle-way. This school developed extensively in India and later on came to Tibet. In Tibet, the teachings were spread mainly by three people who were referred to as "the three" in the historical records. There was Shantarakshita, who was called *khenpo*. Then there was "the guru," who was Padmasambhava. And finally there was the great Tibetan king, Trisong Detsen, who invited the other two to Tibet to build Tibet's first Buddhist monastery, Samye. Together these three made it possible for the teachings to develop in Tibet in the seventh century C.E. But a prophecy by Shantarakshita predicted that there would come a time when the view of the teachings of the Buddha and also the practice would become degraded. He said that at this time, they should request Kamalashila, who was a disciple of Shantarakshita, to come and clarify the teachings.

The prophecy eventually came true. Not long after Shantarakshita had passed away, a teacher from China called Hashang Mahayana came to Tibet. He was extremely well versed in the sutras of the Buddha, but he believed that the "instantaneous path" was superior to the way taught by Shantarakshita. Hashang Mahayana taught that it is irrelevant whether a white cloud or a black cloud obscures the sun, it still veils the sky. Similarly, it is not necessary to be concerned about having virtuous thoughts or unvirtuous thoughts, because they both just obscure one's meditation. His main instruction for meditation was to immerse oneself in the emptiness of meditation and not to worry about accumulating merit. After Hashang Mahayana had propounded these ideas in Tibet, some people said, "I'm following the instantaneous path," while others said, "I'm following the gradual path." This created a great deal of controversy, and the king, Trisong Detsen, remembering Shantarakshita's prophecy, invited Kamalashila to come to Tibet.

Kamalashila thought that he should try to find out what kind of qualities Hashang Mahayana had. If he were intelligent, the best thing would be to debate him. But if he wasn't very clever, Hashang Mahayana would stubbornly stick to his own view and there would be no way to make him change his mind. So Kamalashila decided that he should first examine Hashang Mahayana. It so happened that one day they were both standing on each side of the Brahmaputra River. Kamalashila took the stick he was carrying in his hand and turned it three times above his head. Hashang Mahayana being very intelligent immediately understood the message of this symbolic gesture to mean, "Where do the three dimensions of *conditioned existence* (Skt. *samsara*) come from?" In order to give his answer he just tapped his hands inside his very long sleeves, which were hanging with his hands tucked inside. His answer was, "They come from ignorance, from the dualistic belief in terms of subject and object which obscures the true nature of things." Then Kamalashila understood that this person was in fact intelligent and that he could use logic to defeat him.

Eventually, Kamalashila and Hashang Mahayana met and had a long debate, each one defending his own position, with Hashang Mahayana trying to put forward his idea of the instantaneous path and Kamalashila propounding the idea of the gradual path. In the end Kamalashila defeated Hashang Mahayana. Hashang Mahayana accepted his defeat and returned to China. Before he left, he actually acknowledged his mistaken view, realizing that giving up all notion of what is virtuous and unvirtuous was an incorrect view.

Kamalashila then saw that he would have to show the people of Tibet that the instantaneously path wasn't the correct path. He decided to give them teachings that followed quite closely the meaning of the second turning of the wheel of Dharma. To do this, he wrote a three volume book called *The Stages of Meditation,* in which he described the system of gradual meditation, based on Madhyamaka logic.

There are two main styles of meditation that can be done in regard to the study of emptiness. First one can engage in analytical meditation which involves going into a deep meditation and then intellectually asking questions. The second is placement meditation in which one simply rests in the nature of the mind and "looks" at the mind without any analysis. This gradual path which has been followed in Tibet since the time of Kamalashila has to do mostly with the analytical, or scholar's meditation. This meditation begins with the logical investigation of phenomena in order to conceptually understand their empty nature. Once we have thoroughly investigated the question, we begin to understand how things are actually empty. We can gain gradual conviction about the empty nature of phenomena. Once we are absolutely convinced that all things are empty, we can then engage in placement meditation and begin resting within this conviction. As we train our mind to understand the true nature, we can begin to experience this wisdom in the meditation itself without confusion.

Returning to our story, Kamalashila actually came to Tibet twice. But the second time, he didn't come in the same form. There is an amusing story behind this. Kamalashila was a very handsome man. When he returned to India from Tibet, he came to a place where there had been an epidemic of a dangerous disease. Somebody had died of the disease, but everybody around there was afraid of getting close to the corpse because they didn't want to catch the disease. Kamalashila thought that he must do something to help. Kamalashila was a practitioner of the *phowa* practice, which involves the transference of consciousness. So he left his own beautiful body behind and transferred his mind into the corpse of the dead person. Having animated that corpse with his own mind, he took it to the ocean and threw it in, so it was no longer a risk for anyone. Then his mind left the corpse and went to reenter his own body, but it wasn't to be found. An Indian yogi who was also well versed in the art of transference of consciousness and who happened to be extremely ugly had come by and finding a beautiful corpse on the ground. He thought, "I'm lucky today!" and without hesitation he transferred his consciousness into the beautiful body of Kamalashila and left his ugly body behind. When Kamalashila came back to get his body, he found just the ugly one of the Indian yogi. He had no choice but to enter the ugly body. After that he didn't use his old name Kamalashila, but took the name of Dampa Sangye. Thus the second time he came to Tibet, he came back as a *mahasiddha* called Dampa Sangye.[4]

When Kamalashila came to Tibet in the form of the mahasiddha Dampa Sangye, he still taught the same subject. He taught how to practice so that one could gain an understanding of emptiness, through understanding the Middle-way instructions. This time he also taught mostly what is known as the *chod* practice as a meditation to develop an understanding of emptiness. The chod practice is called "the way to appease all suffering." It uses different visualizations such as imagining all sorts of demons and gods and other kinds of beings in front of you. You then imagine offering them your flesh and blood. Gradually this brings an understanding of the emptiness of self and phenomena. Although Kamalashila appeared to the people in Tibet in a different body and taught a particular form of the chod practice, he was still expounding the same basic teachings on how to understand emptiness through the Middle-way instructions. So these teachings were a continuation of what he had taught before in the physical form of Kamalashila.

Chart 1
The Six Realms of Samsara

Name	As pictured in thangkas	Obstacle
	HIGHER REALMS	
God realm (Skt. *deva*)	The celestial paradises are shown	Pride
Jealous god realm (Skt. *asura*)	The jealous gods involved in conflict with the gods.	Jealousy
	REALM EASIEST TO ATTAIN ENLIGHTENMENT	
Human realm	Human beings in their houses practicing the dharma	The five disturbing emotions
	LOWER REALMS	
Animal realm	Animals on earth	Ignorance
Hungry ghost (Skt. *preta*)	Ghosts with large bellies and very small mouths and necks	Desire
Hell Realm	Beings being tortured in hot and cold realms	Anger

Chapter 2

Compassion in the Middle-way

The meditation system based on the Middle-way that Kamalashila brought on his first trip to Tibet was actually based on the sutras of the Buddha. Kamalashila believed that there were three main paths to achieve Buddhahood. These three paths are: (1) developing compassion, (2) developing bodhichitta, and (3) developing prajna, which is the understanding of emptiness. Two of these, compassion and *bodhichitta*, are developed by the four *preliminary practices*. The third, prajna, is the actual meditation practice on emptiness. According to Kamalashila, these three paths cover all the aspects of practice needed to achieve Buddhahood.

The first aspect of meditation for Kamalashila was compassion. The Buddha describes in several sutras the necessity for the practice of compassion before any other practice. In one sutra it is said, "If one practices or if one tries to develop only one quality, then all the qualities of the Buddha would be in the palm of one's hand." What is this powerful quality? It is great compassion. All *bodhisattvas* must practice compassion. Another sutra says, "Great compassion necessarily comes before any meditation, and the quality of the meditation will depend entirely on whether there is compassion or not."

The Six Meditations on Compassion

How do we meditate on compassion? We meditate on all the beings who are suffering. Then, thinking how they are always suffering with many hardships and troubles, we develop great compassion. The way to meditate on compassion is to envisage the suffering of the beings of the six realms of samsara.[5] First of all we think of the beings in the hell realms. We try to imagine them being constantly tortured by terrific heat or cold. When these tortures are inflicted on them, they feel them as the worst possible suffering. They are just like us; we do not enjoy suffering, but they have to go through immense suffering. Thinking of their unbearable pain, one feels compassion.

The second meditation applies to the hungry ghosts. We think of them as being constantly tormented by unbearable thirst and hunger. In addition, they have to put up with many physical hardships. Thinking of all those beings who suffer in such terrible ways, we develop the feelings of compassion. This is called the meditation of compassion with respect to the suffering of hunger and thirst of the hungry ghosts.

The third form of the meditation applies to animals. We think of the animals and all the difficulties they have to put up with because they are quite ignorant. Because they lack intelligence, their desire, stupidity, and anger are very strong. This is what causes them to be angry at each other, attack each other, and eat each other, which is one of their basic sufferings. They also suffer when they are domesticated animals. Human beings beat them, tie them up, and make them work hard by carrying heavy loads, and they also kill them. When we look around us, we see how animals suffer just as much as we would if we had to go through that. Thinking of how much they have to endure, one feels compassion for them. This is developing compassion towards animals because of their suffering due to stupidity and ignorance.

The fourth way to meditate on compassion applies to human beings. We think of all the different kinds of problems and difficulties that human beings have to put up with; some are imprisoned or tortured or even killed. Although these people were not born in hell, their condition is very similar to that of beings in hell. With that thought in mind, we try to feel compassion for them. Then there are those who are very poor, lacking everything. Although these people were not born as hungry ghosts, they suffer in a similar way, being constantly hungry and thirsty. Thinking of this, we feel compassion towards people in that condition. Finally, there are people who are enslaved, or even if they are not actually slaves, do not have any freedom. Although these people were not born as animals, in fact, their condition is very similar to that of animals. Other people make them work and order them about. Thinking how painful this is, we feel compassion towards them. Finally we wish to be able to help all those different human beings and release them from their suffering and relieve them from that very painful condition.

The fifth way to meditate on compassion applies to the jealous gods. Although they have all the material pleasures that we could wish for, they are still quite unhappy because of what goes on inside their mind. Their jealousy is so strong that they keep envying what others have, and because of this, they never feel at peace or have real happiness. In the end, that feeling of jealousy is so strong that they end up fighting and quarreling violently. This, of course, generates much pain and suffering for them and others. Thinking of this, we feel compassion for them. This is compassion applied to the suffering of fighting and quarreling of the jealous gods.

Finally, the sixth meditation of compassion applies to the gods. Now in the short term it seems that beings in the god realms have the very best possible situation. They have all the pleasures that we could hope for, but unfortunately there is never any feeling of contentment. No matter how much we get, we always want more, so that the gods never actually feel peace of mind. Their minds are never peaceful or stable. They never feel that they have enough; they are unable to enjoy the happiness of peace. Finally, when they die, they have to go through the terrific anxiety and anguish of seeing where they are going to fall next, which is in a lower realm. So thinking of all the sufferings of the gods, we develop a feeling of compassion even for them.

Developing Compassion

It is very hard at first to develop the feeling of compassion for all beings in the abstract. Therefore we have to gradually develop this habit of thinking in terms of compassion for all beings. We have to start somewhere so we begin with showing compassion towards one person. To begin the meditation,[6] we choose one person who is very close to us, someone we love very much, such as someone in our family or a very close friend. We already have the seed of compassion ready to grow in connection with this particular person so all we need to do is to cultivate compassion through meditation.

We think how we would feel if this particular person that we love so much were put through various situations of extreme suffering. We think how much compassion we would have by how much we would want to help them and protect that person from that suffering. If we do this meditation often enough, then we will come to a point when we will feel genuine compassion towards that particular person we have chosen as the object of meditation.

Then we gradually try to expand the scope of our compassion. Once we feel it for one person, we try to apply it to other people. At the beginning we may develop a strong feeling of compassion for our parents or a close friend or our children. Next apply this to someone else. For instance, if we choose another person at random and think that in the same way that we love our children now, we will feel that much love and compassion for others. We think this person who is not very important to us at the moment has been our child many, many times in previous lives. The love and compassion that we feel for our children in this lifetime, we should also be able to feel for that person who has had the very same relationship with us in a past lifetime. Or, if we feel very strong compassion for our parents, we can think that this other person has been as kind to us in the past, as our kind parents are to us in this life. Because they were our parents in a previous lifetime, there is no reason that we cannot feel the same compassion for that person as we feel now for our parents. In the same way, we may really feel strong compassion towards a close friend, feeling strongly that we are ready to do anything to help our friend be free from suffering. Then we can realize that this random person has probably been our friend hundreds or even thousands of times in previous lives. When we realize this, there is no reason to not treat that person any differently from the way we treat our present friend. So by carefully thinking in this way, we try to develop compassion also for that other person.

Once you have managed to cultivate this feeling of compassion with respect to one person, you try to include more and more people. First, we contemplate our compassion towards people whom we love, people in our family or who are in our circle of friends, until we achieve the same feeling of compassion for all of them. Once we have felt this, we try to apply this feeling of compassion towards people who are neither very close to us nor who really like us. Once we can manage this, we will eventually be able to enlarge our compassion towards people whom we really dislike. We do this by realizing that in past lifetimes these people we can't stand have been our very dear parents or very close friends or beloved children; but due to our delusion, we think of them as our enemy. For us to consider them as our enemies is only a mistake on our part, because they have been so close to us and we have loved them so much in the past. Thinking this, we try to apply the same feeling of compassion to these people also.

Finally we come to a point where we try to feel compassion also for all the people in the place where we live. Once we can feel this, we try to expand this towards the north, the east, the south, the west, finally to all directions, thinking that whoever is there should be the object of our compassion. We should feel compassion for everyone because everyone is basically the same, having the same goal, which is to be happy and not to suffer. Since everybody wants the same thing, that is why it would be totally unreasonable to think that we have to have compassion for some people and not for others. We must try to have our compassion go out to everyone without distinction. We must not feel that some people have a special link with us, but other people have never been connected to us, so it's all right to be indifferent towards them. In actual fact, everyone at one point or another has had a very close relationship with us. There isn't one being who hasn't been our parents or a very close friend or a child we loved dearly at one lifetime or another. When we realize this, we can feel that we have a debt of gratitude towards all beings. We have had this feeling of love for them before, and that this is also what we should feel now. It would be wrong to think that we can afford to just reject all those beings and not have any concern for what happens to them. That would be most unsuitable. Rather we should try to develop compassion towards all beings without any exception or limits.

The Meaning of Compassion

We saw previously in this chapter that there are three main aspects in the Middle-way system of meditation. The first is developing compassion. The Tibetan word for compassion is *nyingje*. The first syllable *nying* means "heart," but actually it refers to the mind. The word *nying* means heart, because it is not merely a way of thinking, but comes from within the deepest part of oneself, from one's heart.[7] The second syllable of the word is *je*, which in this context means "protector." So the Tibetan word for compassion means that once we have managed to develop the feeling of true compassion, this attitude of compassion has the power to protect us from difficulties and suffering and it also protects others from their problems and pain. All of this protection from pain and suffering comes from a pure attitude of mind.

Compassion as a Help for One's Self

If we try to achieve well-being in a selfish way, we have to do it on our own. There won't be anyone else to help us along, since all we are looking for is personal profit and achievement. To achieve personal well being can only be done at other people's expense. Since no one likes something done at their expense, others won't like what we're doing and will try to prevent us from achieving happiness. This creates a great many adverse conditions for us. On the other hand, if we are not working just for our own selfish happiness, but are concerned for others' well-being, then others will recognize this loving concern in us. They will be aware of the fact that we are really trying to express love. If we love them, then they will love us, too. This in turn will benefit us, because other people will recognize that we are trying to help them, and in return they will be prepared to help us. They will see that we are befriending them and they will in turn befriend us. So in the end we will have all the right conditions that we need to achieve our goal, and we will not meet with any obstacles or adverse conditions.

Let's take an example of this. If we don't feel any love for other people, then automatically they will be aware that we don't feel love for them. So that even when we try to talk to them, they will have a feeling that perhaps we are trying to deceive them. When it comes to action, they may feel that we are going to hurt them. They will have this impression that somehow we are going to create an obstacle to their well-being and happiness. So there will always be a feeling of fear and distrust. These people will never become our friends and will never become close, because they feel that there is no love there.

On the other hand, if we are always loving, others will immediately feel that love and will know that we love them. They will know that if the time comes when they need help, they will get help. They will know that they have nothing to fear, that we are not going to hurt or deceive them. This will generate a feeling of mutual friendliness, with a wish to help each other. There will never be a feeling that we might be an enemy, or that we might hurt them, but there will be an automatic feeling that things will go very well between us. Therefore, if we have a loving attitude, others will feel it and will return this love.

If we are able to love one person, that one person will be our friend. If we can love two people, these two people will be our friends. They will help us to achieve what we want to achieve and get rid of obstacles that will prevent us from achieving it. If we love three people or four or six or a hundred or a thousand or 100,000 people, all of these people will be our friends and will help us achieve what we want to achieve and help us get rid of hindrances to our goal. In fact the degree to which we are able to have compassion will determine the degree to which other people can help us and befriend us. So how much we feel love and compassion towards others will be how much benefit and help we will receive from them.

Compassion as a Help for Others

Besides being of benefit for oneself, compassion can truly protect and help other beings. We may not be able to always achieve great things to help other beings, but even if we can't, merely having compassion will already make a tremendous difference. As we just said, if someone has no compassion, no feeling of love for other beings, others will feel this instinctively. They know that this person might cause them trouble, that this person probably won't help them if they need help, creating a constant feeling of fear or apprehension. The mind can never be completely at rest and peaceful because there is this constant feeling of unease. We are preoccupied because we do not know what to expect from the other person.

But if someone has compassion, immediately people can sense that this person is ready to help them if the need arises. When someone meets a truly compassionate person, it is like finding *healing nectar*. Even when one hears the words of someone, who is really compassionate, one can feel that they come from the heart, and this is enough to make one feel very happy. It is enough to make one forget one's suffering, troubles, and problems. One may say this is only a temporary benefit, but whether a temporary or an ultimate benefit, people know there is someone who is thinking in terms of helping them. Just knowing this is like healing nectar. Compassion is the kind of feeling that can only bring something good. It will never generate something harmful.

Compassion is beneficial in the short term and it is also beneficial in the long term. Whether others or we have compassion, this can only be the root of goodness and happiness. At the present, there might not be great benefits coming out of our compassion. Whether we can actually generate something great from our compassion or not, what matters is that the root is there. This root of compassion is bound to bring very good results, something positive. It cannot be the source of defeat or something negative. In the short term, somebody might be able to do something that appears beneficial, but if this action is not backed by compassion, it might very well turn into deception or something that is not pure or completely beneficial. Even if we do something very small and this act is accompanied by compassion from the beginning to the end of the act, there will never be any problems involved with this activity because the activity is completely pure, completely wholesome, all the way through. That is why compassion is good all around. It is good in the short term. It really helps everybody and makes things better for everybody. It is good in the long run too because it is the only thing that will always bring a positive result, never a negative or painful result.

Compassion as the Root of Enlightenment

Compassion has the power to protect oneself and other beings from suffering. The Buddha and all the great bodhisattvas have said again and again how important, how fundamental, this quality of compassion is. What they said is indeed true. Actually, whether they said it or not would not make any difference insofar as compassion itself is concerned. Compassion has this power of protection. Because the Buddha praised compassion does not make the qualities of compassion any greater nor if the Buddha had not praised compassion, his silence would not have made compassion lose its power. Compassion itself has a particular power. This is true even in non-spiritual terms: Compassion can help to protect us from suffering. But, of course, it is even more important in spiritual terms. All the *shravakas*, all the *arhats*, were able to achieve their realization because of the Buddha's teaching. It was through the activity of the Buddha that they were able to achieve realization. And where did the Buddha himself come from? Buddhahood is achieved through three kinds of qualities—compassion, prajna, and bodhichitta. Without these three there is no Buddhahood. However, the root of bodhichitta and prajna is compassion. Bodhichitta and prajna develop from a foundation of compassion, so the root of all achievements in Dharma and the spiritual path is compassion.

Compassion is not necessarily very strong in our mind at first. Nor is it very stable at the beginning, so we have to practice in order to develop compassion. We know that without compassion there will be many problems, many difficulties for ourselves and for others. That is why we have to practice to develop our compassion more and more.

Developing Compassion

What is the main way to develop compassion? It's done in two steps. The first step is to try to see within ourselves a person we feel compassion for—our parents or our children or a friend. To find a single person we have compassion for is a very important thing. Once we have found that first little spark of compassion, we try to develop it more and more, so that it can become more and more beneficial for others and for ourself. Once we develop our compassion, other people will feel this compassion in us. They will be able to taste that feeling of compassion in us and this will make them feel happy. In return, they will feel compassion towards us. Then there will be a sort of exchange of compassion going back and forth between us. This will develop the compassion greater and greater, and will become a greater source of happiness all the time. This is how we try to develop compassion, starting with one very small aspect of compassion that is already there in us.

We begin by feeling compassion for all the people we are very close to. Then we try to extend it to people we know in general but with whom we have no particularly close relationship, and then we extend it even to people we don't know. Finally, we generate compassion towards those we dislike or even people who are trying to harm us. Normally, we feel anger and aggression towards the person we consider our enemy, but we should realize that anger is really a very tricky thing because anger becomes so unbearable that we have to do something to hurt the other person. But if we follow through with our anger, it will not only be harmful for the other person, but it will also be for us as well because once we start hurting the other person, his anger is going to flare up like a fire. Once he is angry at us, whatever we do will be hindered by what he is doing to stop us and we won't be able to find the right conditions to do what we have to do. This in turn will make our anger flare up again. From that time onwards, it will be a constant escalation of harm between the two of us, until in the end it will be totally out of control. It just goes on and on without limit. That is why we should try not to resort to anger.

What should we do in the face of anger? If somebody else hurts us, we should try to understand that the other person doesn't really know what he or she is doing. If we can generate this feeling of compassion when somebody else is hurting us, then automatically his anger will tend to decrease. If the next time around, we are able to feel compassionate, his anger will become even less than before. If we continue doing this, he may even come to like us in the end. So it is very beneficial if we can avoid being angry. Once we have managed to develop compassion with respect to those who dislike us, we will be able to extend that feeling of compassion to all beings wherever they are in the world.

We try to develop compassion more and more through repeated practice. At first we begin with one person and in the end we extend our compassion to millions and millions of beings. In fact we embrace everyone because every sentient being has the same desire to find happiness and be free from suffering. Our compassion should end up being towards all without any exception or any bias.

At first we should concentrate on great and obvious suffering. Then we apply ourselves to minor forms of suffering. Then we apply ourselves not just to suffering itself, but also to its cause, which is unvirtuous action. For instance, we begin to realize that even when people are not actually suffering at the moment, they are creating the cause of future suffering through doing unvirtuous actions. It is like watching someone approaching an abyss; even though the person hasn't fallen in it yet, we know it could occur at any time.

Then we can develop compassion for beings because they do not understand the truth of reality. Compassion will develop more and more and become finer and finer until it becomes compassion without any conceptual reference. So we try to develop compassion progressively, until it reaches that final stage.

To summarize, the main point in the system of Middle-way meditation is to meditate in order to understand the true nature of things and to develop the conviction that the nature of things is empty. But before we discuss the actual subject matter of the Middle-way, it is necessary to develop compassion in order to achieve this realization. That is why compassion is the preliminary practice for the actual meditation of the Middle-way.

Questions

Question: Could you please explain karmic obscurations?

Rinpoche: As you know there are three main obscurations: the emotional obscurations, the cognitive obscurations, and the karmic obscurations. The karmic obscurations mean simply that when you act in a wrong way such as killing out of anger, stealing out of desire or whatever, you accumulate all sorts of negative karma. Once you have accumulated that much bad karma, you will be reborn in a lower realm. If you are born in the hell realms or as a hungry ghost or an animal, you won't have the opportunity to hear the Dharma and practice it.

For example, even if you were born as an animal, such as an ox, in Bodhgaya at the time of the Buddha, it wouldn't help you very much because you couldn't really feel any faith towards the Buddha or make use of his teachings. In this sense, these beings are obscured by their own karma. This is what stops them from being able to practice. On the other hand, somebody who hasn't accumulated that much negative karma can be reborn as a human being and as such will have the opportunity to practice the Dharma.

Question: Couldn't the nirmanakaya manifest as an ox?

Rinpoche: Of course, there are forms of the emanation of the Buddha that can manifest as animals, but we were speaking of what is called the supreme nirmanakaya, which we usually call the historical Buddha. An ox or any other animal couldn't benefit from the presence of the historical Buddha. This isn't the fault of the nirmanakaya. It is the fault of the being. There is a Tibetan saying that if you have a cave that is facing north, that cave will never receive any sunshine inside. This condition isn't because the sun isn't shining; it is just that the cave is facing north, so it just doesn't get any sunlight. In the same way, even though the supreme nirmana-kaya may be there and teaching and benefiting all beings without any partiality, if the beings are not able to be receptive to the teachings, they are not able to benefit from them.

Question: If you develop compassion with respect to other beings, you have to relate to them in quite a close way. Isn't this going to create attachment? Isn't it better to just be on your own and do your practice and try to develop compassion in that way?

Rinpoche: We have to distinguish between what is love and what is attachment. These two questions might look quite similar, but they are in fact very different in their essence. When there is real love, real loving concern, or real loving kindness, there is a very pure motivation that leads to very pure action. This stems from a wish to really help the other person with his problems and suffering, and a genuine wish to help him or her to find happiness and well-being. Attachment may look very similar to love, but behind it there is always an expectation of some form of reward or profit for oneself. Because of this expectation, it isn't a very positive quality. Here we are speaking of trying to develop real loving kindness, real love, not attachment. If we can develop that aspect, it will be beneficial all the way through. This can inspire us to practice the Dharma for the sake of all other beings. If we don't try to develop this, then there is always the risk of falling into the *hinayana* style of practice.

Question: Is there a particular meditation on a particular deity that is particularly beneficial in understanding the Middle-way?

Rinpoche: There are lots of different meditations, but in fact they all have the same purpose. There are meditations on some deities in order to increase our capacity to understand emptiness, compassion, or bodhichitta. But basically because they all stem from these same basic points, when we begin to meditate, it doesn't really matter on which deity we meditate because they all lead to the same thing.

Question: Isn't there a problem with being too compassionate?

Rinpoche: When we try to practice compassion, it doesn't immediately have to be the ultimate form of compassion. It has to be a gradual practice. Sometimes we might feel spontaneously like doing something, but we have to try to see the implications of what we are doing. Would it really benefit others in the long term, because what we think might help right away might not help later on. We might not be able to keep it up. Maybe difficulties we have not foreseen might show up because we didn't think enough. So we have to be careful, being compassionate according to our own capabilities and our own understanding. There is a Tibetan proverb that says, "When somebody is very new in the practice of compassion, he will give butter to a dog." On the other hand when someone is a very seasoned meditator, he or she might make the mistake of turning into very tough leather. So we can make mistakes in both ways, either because we're too new and overdo it, or we might have practiced a lot, so we become a lot harder than when we started. So there are two kinds of mistakes that can be made in relation to compassion.

The Middle-way Meditation Instructions

Chapter 3

Bodhichitta in the Middle-way

In the last chapter we saw that the system of meditation of the Middle-way covers three aspects. The first is compassion, the second is bodhichitta, and the third is the development of the understanding of emptiness through prajna. All these stages have to be practiced one after the other. For each stage it is a matter of increasing the respective qualities by developing them more and more. In the last chapter we saw that we begin by applying compassion to one person, and this grows greater and greater until we embrace all beings. So it's a matter of always trying to develop the quality of compassion according to how much determination and how much effort we can produce.

It isn't quite enough to remain within this feeling of compassion. We must go one step further to develop bodhichitta, the mind's intent on enlightenment. What is the essence of bodhichitta? It is actually compassion, but it is compassion that has been developed so much that it has come to the essence of bodhichitta. We shouldn't think that first we must try to develop compassion and then some day we can forget all about compassion and jump into this new thing which is bodhichitta. Rather the final development of compassion is bodhichitta.

Compassion is the attitude that makes us want to relieve the suffering of other beings, because we realize that other beings have to endure all sorts of pain and troubles and experience constant fear and apprehension. Compassion is the wish to help them out of this situation. So in this sense, compassion is like medicine, like healing nectar (Skt. *amrita*). But this type of compassion does not go far enough because there has to be the actual practice, an action that follows this intention. This practice is to help others be free from suffering and find happiness. Only then is compassion really effective. Otherwise, it is just a very noble attitude not bearing much fruit. For example, imagine that a bird falls to the ground because it's sick. You find that bird and you feel compassion towards it, so you feed it and look after it. Perhaps the bird will get better, but perhaps it will die. Anyway it is very good of you to have this feeling of compassion, because you are helping the bird with its pain and suffering. But this kind act doesn't eliminate all of the bird's suffering because the bird will still have hardships later on. This physically caring for the bird isn't complete because you haven't managed to eliminate all of its suffering. That bird will still have difficulties and suffering to endure. Take another example of a fish that has ended up on dry land. You see the fish suffering and you throw the fish back into the water. Once again this is a very good thing to do because it will take away the immediate cause of suffering for the fish. But this action isn't complete, because the fish still has lots of other suffering to go through. In the same way, if we give someone who is sick some medicine, this is going to help relieve the pain at that particular moment, but when the person gets well that person will still have lots of difficulties to endure. In this sense, whatever we can do on the basis of such good intentions is very, very good; but it is not quite enough. We must prepare for something even greater than this, which is to aim at relieving all suffering for good. This is really the greatest kind of motivation and the one that will be the most beneficial.

Normally, we think of compassion with respect to the people, the animals and the beings that we can see around us. We think this person is suffering, so we try to help. If we see someone sick or poor or suffering, we have this very generous, very good feeling that we want to help relieve that person's suffering. This is indeed a very good thought that will bear great results, both for ourself and for others. But, in fact, it is not quite enough in the sense we see only a handful among the billions and billions of beings everywhere that are suffering. Also many of those other billions are in a much worse situation than those we can actually see. We cannot afford to think we can help just the ones we can see and forget all the others. Somehow we must try to expand our compassion to embrace all the other beings, even the ones we don't see, because there are so many others who suffer in much worse ways. So our compassion must become much greater in terms of the number of beings to whom it is applied.

We must try to think in terms of relieving the suffering of all beings without any exception. This, of course, should apply also to beings who presently seem happy, but will be unhappy later on. We must have the attitude of helping those beings also. But it is important that our compassion both in intention and in action shouldn't be what is called a "mixed" type of compassion, in which in order to help one being we have to harm another being. It is like seeing a dog that is starving and out of compassion for the dog, catching a fish to feed the dog. This is not the right kind of compassion because in the immediate term we help the dog; but we also kill the fish. It isn't genuine compassion because in order to help one, we had to hurt another.

Genuine compassion is good from beginning to end and does not involve hurting anyone in the process. The very fact that it can be beneficial relies on the purity of the action throughout. Any genuine compassionate action will never bring anything painful or negative to another.

We must develop the right kind of compassion, so that, little by little, through compassionate action we can help protect beings from their suffering. To do this we must help them avoid the cause of suffering and prevent them from hurting one another. This is to lead them gradually on the way to liberation, because once liberation is achieved, suffering will finally and completely be eliminated. Therefore, compassion has to be developed, but the kind of compassion that is intelligent enough to be applied in the right way.

Bodhichitta

When our compassion reaches its highest level, it is called bodhichitta (Tib. *chang chup kyi sem*).[8] This is the desire to achieve enlightenment for the sake of all beings. It is the understanding that all beings will end all their suffering when they achieve enlightenment. So once compassion has become complete, it automatically turns into bodhichitta.

As long as we are ordinary beings (that is, unenlightened persons) we cannot actually practice bodhichitta. We can only start developing that state of mind, but we can't actually free beings yet. This ability to free beings will only occur once we have achieved enough realization and the right view for our actions. As long as we are ordinary beings, sometimes we understand, sometimes we don't; sometimes we do things right, sometimes we don't. If we were to actually try to practice bodhichitta at this moment, it would be like the blind leading the blind, which usually ends up with both falling into an abyss. Before we can actually help beings in the great sense, we need our own clear vision. That is, we have to eliminate all of our own defects and develop all of our good qualities to achieve the realization of Buddhahood.

First, we have to develop genuine compassion. Then we must increase this more and more until it is really complete and we have achieved bodhichitta, which is based on this very pure compassionate motivation. Actually even if we cannot practice bodhichitta, we can still have the motivation to help others which is extremely good and valuable. The Buddha in one of the sutras illustrated this point with an example. He said if one has a diamond ring, even with a piece broken off it, that diamond ring will still be better than, for example, a gold ring. It will still be more valuable because the diamond is so precious. In the same way, possessing true bodhichitta is the very best state of mind. Even though one is unable to put it into action, this intention in itself is so pure, so great, that it is more valuable than the actual practice of the shravaka practitioners who follow the hinayana path of self realization for their own benefit. Even though shravakas do an actual practice, it is less valuable than the mere intention of bodhichitta. Bodhichitta in this sense is like the diamond, even though it is not entirely complete, it is still a valuable intention. A practice, which is based on self-concern, will not give a great result, whereas whatever is based on the pure bodhichitta intention will give very great results. That is why the view of bodhichitta is said to be so vast.

The final outcome of compassion is bodhichitta, which has two aspects. One aspect is the wish and the other aspect is the action. When we begin, we cannot actually put bodhichitta into practice. It remains a wish, with us thinking, "May I be able one day to help all beings be free from their suffering forever. May I be able to help them find happiness forever." So it is a desire that the day will come when we can actually do this. This wish is also completely impartial and unbiased, applying to all beings without exception. Once the wish is fully developed, it turns into an action of actually working towards enlightenment. The way this is done is thinking in terms of "I must achieve Buddhahood, so I can really be able to help beings, I must increase this power, in order to help beings."

When both the wish and the practice toward enlightenment are found together, then this is the seed of the power to remove the suffering of others and achieve Buddhahood for oneself. The Buddha in one of his teachings said, "Noble sons and daughters the seed that gives birth to all the qualities of the Buddhas is bodhichitta." Bodhichitta can give birth to those qualities both in oneself and in others. It is not just a tiny seed that will give birth to one fruit, but it is an extraordinary seed that will bear billions and billions of fruits. Bodhichitta will generate the qualities of Buddhahood for oneself and others. These are the great benefits of bodhichitta, and becoming aware of them, we will try to develop this noble state of mind.

The actual subject matter of Middle-way meditation is the meditation on emptiness that lets us realize the true nature of all things. Before we actually practice the meditation on emptiness, we have to practice compassion and bodhichitta. It is necessary to have this right kind of attitude and to develop it sufficiently so that the meditation on emptiness will come naturally to us. If at the beginning we try to force ourselves to meditate by thinking, "I must meditate, I must do it," we will most likely encounter a great number of obstacles and probably won't be able to complete the meditation. We won't feel happy about meditating, we won't feel any real incentive to do it, and we won't feel any enthusiasm about it. It will be more like a dictator saying, "You must meditate now, you must do it now," and thus not produce many results. However, if we first develop compassion towards all other beings, this gives birth to the pure motivation of bodhichitta, and as a result, we will want to achieve enlightenment in order to help other beings. Because of bodhichitta we will really want to realize the nature of phenomena, because we know that this is the way to help other beings. Then the wish to meditate will come very naturally. It will be like a fire that catches automatically on nice dry wood. Nobody will have to come and push you from behind. You will just want to do it yourself.

This is the way the system of Middle-way meditation works. First of all one needs the basis or ground, which is the practice of compassion. Then when one's compassion has sufficiently increased, it becomes bodhichitta. This bodhichitta has to be cultivated until one is ready for the meditation on emptiness.

Sending and Taking Practice

When beginning meditation, one of the ways to increase bodhichitta and compassion is the practice of *sending and taking* (Tib. *tong len*). In this meditation one thinks that one is taking in others' suffering and the causes of their suffering; in exchange one gives them one's happiness and causes of happiness. We may ask if we can really transfer to others the causes of our happiness. Actually, we can't in real terms, but what we are trying to do through this meditation is to develop the root, the seed of the actual ability to do this in the future. The seed of this is compassion, bodhichitta. With this meditation we are trying to reinforce our bodhichitta which can be compared to a healing nectar or medicine. It has, in fact, an important effect that is to increase our compassion and bodhichitta. The degree to which we manage to increase and develop compassion will determine the degree to which we are actually able to help other beings. So if somebody says, "With that meditation can you really take away the suffering of beings?" the answer is "Not in the short term, but in the long term, yes." This is why one practices this meditation.

Some people have worries about this form of meditation. They think that by imagining or visualizing giving happiness to others, they give away their own happiness and lose it. They also believe that by imagining that they are taking on other beings' suffering, all that misery and suffering are going to pile up on them to the point that the suffering becomes totally unbearable. But there is no need to be worried, because nothing is really going to happen. In fact, this way of thinking occurs because we have become so used to thinking in an egotistical way. It is very natural that we should feel this way at the beginning, but we should understand that there is really no danger of losing our happiness and receiving a lot of suffering. Sending and taking meditation is not like trading because we are not actually exchanging anything in real terms. We don't have the power to make things happen so quickly in terms of cause and effect. But we might ask, "If there is nothing happening, what is the point? Why should I bother to meditate in this way if I can't really take away any suffering, and if I can't give away my happiness?" But there is a point to this meditation in that although we aren't doing a real exchange now, we are developing compassion and bodhichitta, developing them to the point where later on they will bring forth the real ability to help in such a way. This practice is the basis for later becoming capable of taking away other beings' suffering and giving them happiness. That is why it is such a meaningful and important practice.

Most of us probably know the meditation on sending and taking, but for those who don't, the basic principle is that sending and taking are synchronized with the breathing. When breathing out, we imagine that we send out bright white light. This bright white light goes out to all beings, who are visualized before us. When this white light touches them, we think that all our happiness and the causes of happiness are now with them. We think that they feel genuinely happy and content. When we inhale, we think that all the suffering, all the pain, all the worries, troubles, and negativity of all beings are coming into us in the form of a blackish light. When this light comes into us, we think that now all those beings are free from all their problems and suffering and that they feel very happy.

The Middle-way Meditation Instructions

Chapter 4

Prajna in the Middle-way

Before discussing the actual techniques of the meditation of the Middle-way or Madhyamaka, we have discussed the three causal conditions for this meditation: compassion, bodhichitta, and prajna. In the previous two chapters we have discussed compassion and bodhichitta; in this chapter we will discuss wisdom or prajna.[9] In the previous chapter, we saw the different ways in which we can develop bodhichitta, the very pure intention to help all beings. When this motivation has developed completely, the intention becomes action and we actually become capable of helping beings, not just wishing that we could help them. With full development of prajna all our actions are done with intelligence, with understanding, with the quality of prajna. This is why prajna is described as being the means to enter the path.

Prajna will have to be developed through different stages. First we develop this understanding through study. When we have studied enough, we develop the understanding that comes from contemplation. Finally, we develop the higher aspect of understanding, wisdom, which comes through meditation.

We said before that we need the right kind of motivation, which is compassion and bodhichitta. But this pure motivation also has to be accompanied by understanding. This is necessary not only in spiritual situations, but also in ordinary life. Whatever we do, we need to know what we are doing; otherwise we won't be able to quickly accomplish what we are doing or complete it. There has to be a basic understanding of the situation. If there is an understanding of the situation, what we are doing will work out properly and quickly. In all respects, we need this form of understanding or intelligence. Basically we have the pure motivation of compassion and bodhichitta through which we want to help everyone find happiness and be free from suffering. This is a very difficult task, but it is a very noble one. In order to achieve it, we need even more intelligence than when doing any other kind of action. We need to know just what we are doing and to understand what is happening. That is why it is so very important to develop the quality of prajna, the first step in developing prajna is to study.

Listening to the Teachings

To develop prajna or intelligence, we must first listen to the teachings, second contemplate them, and third meditate on them. We begin by listening to the teachings. In previous times this meant simply listening to the Dharma as spoken by our teacher. In a more modern context, it means to study the teachings. Why is this necessary at all? We and all other beings from beginningless samsara have always been in search of the same thing, trying to be happy and eliminate all suffering and difficulties. Although we have been trying for so long, somehow we haven't been able to achieve this. We haven't been able to fulfill our hopes and our wishes. Although we don't want suffering, we keep on encountering it. Although we want happiness so much, we haven't managed to find it because we do not know the right way to achieve happiness and freedom from suffering. We don't understand the principles of how to create happiness so we can't achieve what we are looking for. We may think, "Up to now I was mistaken, but perhaps now I'll find a way." However since what we have been doing in the past was a mistake, we are probably going to make the same mistake now, and again this will give the wrong results. The right thing to do is to find a person who has had some experience in the right way to find happiness. Once we know that this person has actually achieved happiness for himself or herself, we can try the same means, the same path, to achieve the same result.

As an example, if you have been trying to go somewhere unknown and you've taken the wrong road, made many mistakes, and never reached your destination, you just carry on and most likely you will become even more lost. However, if you find someone who has traveled the road before and is able to show you the way, you will get there all right. The person who has the experience of the road to truly finding happiness and eliminating suffering is the

Buddha. He found the right way and through this he was able to achieve the ultimate realization. Once he obtained this experience himself, he taught it to others so that they could do the same themselves.

So we have to learn from what the Buddha has explained very clearly so we will no longer remain ignorant about how to achieve happiness and eliminate suffering. This is why we first have to develop understanding through study, to develop prajna.

When the Buddha gave teachings, he didn't just say, "You mustn't do this, you must do that." Rather, each time he explained what he meant with very precise reasons for why one should act in this way and avoid acting in that way. Following the Buddha wasn't just a matter of believing him out of respect or practicing out of blind faith, because that would not have developed prajna in his students. The whole point of the path is to develop understanding within oneself. That is why the Buddha always explained the reason for doing something. Each time the Buddha said that it is good to practice this or to have this kind of attitude, he pointed out the reasons by showing the advantages or disadvantages in doing that particular thing. The Buddha emphasized that we should try to generate the right kind of motivation from beginning the path until the final realization of enlightenment. In *The Jewel Ornament of Liberation* Gampopa describes the way to practice the path and the way to acquire the various *bodhisattva levels* of realization. He also discusses the true nature of phenomena and the reasons why phenomenon are empty. We learn about all this by actually receiving teachings from a spiritual friend and by reading the Buddha's teachings. So, these teachings are the way we can find out what is the right path shown by the Buddha and the reasons behind it. Through learning this, we can develop our own understanding. In summary, this is the first step that will lead to the development of prajna, true knowing.

The transmission of these Middle-way teachings comes from the Buddha's teaching. We shouldn't think that they were written by some great scholars, with their own theories, because what the Middle-way scholars did was to take the profound words of the Buddha and make them more accessible; that is, easier to understand, easier to memorize, and easier to relate to. They didn't introduce things that the Buddha hadn't said nor did they change things that the Buddha had said. They left the Buddha's teachings as they were, but just made them easier for others to understand.

We need to study the teachings of the Buddha and his followers to assimilate the profound meaning of the Buddha's teachings. All of this leads us onto the stainless path taught by the Buddha. There isn't any difference between the teachings given by scholars in the commentaries (Skt. *shastra*) and those given in the Buddha's own words (Skt. *sutra*). But after study we must begin another practice—contemplation.

Contemplating the Teachings

To develop the second aspect of prajna is to reflect on or contemplate the meaning of the teachings. During this stage of study, one is concentrating on the texts and the spoken teachings. At the same time, one has to absorb the words and the actual meaning of the teachings. After the study of the teachings, there has to be a phase of reflection where one tries to ascertain the meaning of the teachings. This goes on until one develops a really strong conviction about the validity of the teachings which is done first through considering the scriptures and the reasons they give, and second through one's own reasoning.

First we read through the scriptures themselves, considering all the reasons given in the teachings. Then we use our own logic to find out whether what is taught is actually valid or not. We have to examine the scriptures very closely. The example of refining gold is always used for describing this process. Before we can have pure gold, we have to heat it to a high temperature in a fire, then we have to beat it, and so on until we obtain pure gold. In the same way, we must examine the teachings thoroughly and repeatedly until we come to the conviction of their validity. We can understand what is expounded in the teachings without any doubt or mistake. This second phase of development of prajna is done through reflection on the scriptures and through using our own discernment.

Meditating on the Teachings

The third aspect of developing prajna is to meditate on the teachings. There are two main styles of meditation. One style is the analytical meditation (Tib. *je gom*) of the scholar in which we examine things through intellectual reflection. The other is the placement meditation (Tib. *jo gom*) of the yogis. This is the meditation of directly looking into mind to see the true nature of mind.[10] The meditation of the yogi can bring results very quickly, but it is not easy to describe.

The meditation of the scholar,[11] or *pandita,* provides a very firm, very clear basis for the practice. Once you have developed that clear basis, you can't make any mistake. Whatever you are going to consider will be very clear, valid, true, without any doubt and with definite conviction. You won't find yourself in a situation where you think, "It could be like this or it could be like that."

In contrast, in the style of a yogi of placement meditation there are times when you aren't quite sure what is going on, what is understood or not understood. Then you have to rely on the *blessings*[12] of the guru to actually realize the nature of mind. By contrast, the scholar's meditation is a matter of knowing things for what they are. You know what exists just as it is. This is what gives you great confidence, great certainty. In fact, there are two steps in the process. The first step is looking outside to get the knowledge of what you are seeking. You are learning from the texts, from the sutras and shastras to gain some kind of conviction of what it is. This corresponds to the first stage of listening. Then in the reflection phase, you turn inwards. You are starting to look at the texts in a much more introspective way because you try to ascertain their validity for yourself through the reasons given in the scriptures and through your own critical faculty. This is how you develop the side of prajna that comes through reflection. The result of this process of reflection is that you come to a degree of certainty that will not be altered by anything. It is a certainty that does not depend on anybody else. It comes only from your own personal, proper examination of the teachings, which leads you to unflinching conviction. Once you know the teachings are correct, nothing can make you change your mind. You don't need anybody else to tell you how things are. You have formed your own conviction on the basis of the teachings themselves. Even if the Buddha were to come along and say that it isn't like this, you wouldn't change your mind because you have reached a point where there is no longer any doubt. Your conviction and certainty are complete.

Another way in which your certainty is complete is that nobody can make you feel that you are wrong, that you are mistaken in your belief, because you know for yourself that the reasons given in the scriptures and your own judgment have proved the validity of the teachings. This is what can give you such a clear certainty about what you have learned. Now this certainty will also be extended to realizing the actual nature of everything. You will be able to gain this conviction concerning the ultimate nature of things through examining the causes and effects of all things.

It is necessary to have certainty about something through examination, because this is what leads you to the kind of understanding which allows no room for mistakes or doubts. Sometimes it's possible to know something, but if you don't know it in such a way that it is clear enough and certain enough, you may still have doubts, and this may destroy your initial belief and understanding. There is a story that can be a good illustration of this point. One day there was a Brahmin who was walking along with a goat. He was going to make an offering with this goat. Three robbers came along who decided they would find a way to steal the goat from that Brahmin. The first robber went up to the Brahmin and said, "Hello. Where are you going with this dog? Why are you taking this dog along with you?" The Brahmin looked at him a bit surprised and thought, "Well, he's talking rubbish. I'm not taking any dog along. I've got a goat." He thought the man was a bit strange so he kept on walking. Then a few minutes later the second robber walked up to the Brahmin and says, "Oh, what are you doing, taking this dog along like this?" Then the Brahmin started to think, "What's going on? First that man comes along and asks me why I'm taking a dog and now this other one comes too and says that I'm taking a dog along." The Brahmin thought that it was a bit strange. So he started to become a bit doubtful about what he really was taking along with him. He wanted to reassure himself, so he looked at the goat and saw the horns and so forth and said, "Yeah, it's really a goat. I don't understand why they are going on about a dog." Then the third robber came along, and said, "Hello Brahmin. What are you doing taking a dog along like this." This time it was a bit too much. "What's going on now? I say "goat," but everybody else says "dog." There must be something wrong. Maybe there is some foul play or some demon somewhere. It's getting too much now." He decided to just leave the goat behind, because he couldn't stand it. This goes to show if you don't examine things with enough intelligence, you can't stick to what you have understood to be the truth. You can't stick to it because you don't have enough critical sense to know that what you understood in the first place was right. That is why you need to examine things properly, in a discerning way, in order to get the kind of certainty that cannot change and the certainty that what you know actually is the truth.

The Reasoning of Cause

In order to develop real conviction, one has to examine, using reasoning, where things come from, what are the causes of things, and what are the effects. If one says that there is no cause for anything, this simply isn't true. It's easy to see that a seedling or a shoot came from a seed. Besides the seed, which was the cause, many different conditions were required, such as soil, fertilizer, water, and so on. If there wasn't a cause for everything, then one could get a crop in the winter, a crop inside the house without any soil, or whatever. Things would just happen at random.

For everything to happen there has to be a cause. There can be two kinds of causes: permanent causes and impermanent causes. Some philosophies and religions believe the world has been created by a creator or a god. The belief in a creator implies that every change in this world is due to the creator. The creator has to create the causes for the effects that we see in this world. However, if we look at the beginning of the creation, we see this is impossible. If we believe in a creator, then the creator must have made all the causes for the effects of the world we live in. However, the world we live in is impermanent, and things are being made all the time. So the causes for the world to arise cannot be permanent. But if the cause is impermanent, this brings us to the three aspects of time: the past, present, and future. The past is something that has gone. Since it is no longer, how can the past ever affect anything? The past cannot do anything because it is gone. What we did last year is not here any more, so it cannot do anything in the present. Now, concerning the future, the future is not here yet, so how can it affect anything just now? It doesn't exist now. What is left is the present. Is the present actually doing something, having a function? Well, the present is a very small thing, if anything at all. Because even if we consider this instant, which is the present instant, it very quickly becomes the past, the previous instant. Very quickly the next instant is coming, so even if we are speaking of the present instant, it's only a very short period of time, if anything at all. So we can't really expect that the present instant can generate and create everything.

In this way we can begin to understand that things do not originate without a cause. Likewise, they do not originate from a permanent cause or from an impermanent cause, which leads us to the conclusion that all things never even started to exist; they have never originated. In other words, they are by nature empty. However, since we are under the influence of the illusion that things are solid and real, we see things manifesting in all sorts of different ways. The Buddha said in the *Heart Sutra,* "Form is empty." This is because the objects which we see in various forms are by nature empty, in the sense that they never started to exist. They never arose, so the Buddha in the next line said, "Emptiness is form." The form that manifests to us in so many different ways is essentially nonexistent, unreal, but while it is empty, it does manifest in a form, so this form is actually the form of emptiness. Emptiness is form. Then the Buddha said, "There is no form separate from emptiness." This shows that emptiness and form are of one and the same essence. They are completely inseparable. It is similar to what happens when we are dreaming. If we dream about an elephant, this elephant does not exist. If we consider its essence, there is no real elephant there. It does not exist. There is an absence of elephant, but still you see an elephant. The nonexistence the elephant and our seeing the elephant are not two separate things. They are one. In this example, we can begin to understand how the nature of all things is empty. The point of the second stage of the prajna of reflection is to develop conviction in the emptiness of all external phenomena.

We have seen that, through the process of reflection, we come to a definite certainty. This certainty has been elaborated through investigation, through thinking, and through examination, but once this certainty exists, then all we need to do is remain within this lucid, clear certainty and just meditate within that. This is the way to develop understanding that comes out of meditation. This is the way to develop the finest aspect of prajna. By doing this, our understanding will become clearer and clearer, more and more stable.

Questions

Question: I did not understand the reasoning about a permanent cause. Could you say some more about this?

Rinpoche: When we say that something is permanent, it implies that it doesn't change. But when we speak of effects or results, this usually is the result of a change and results are not constant. Sometimes something may be there, sometimes it may not be there. For instance, we will get crops in the summer, but will not get any crops in the winter. Now if the cause were permanent, there would always be a result all the time. We would have a crop in the winter, we would have a crop in the summer, we will have it all the time, since the cause would be there permanently, always producing a result. Whereas if we said the cause were absent, we would never get a result. There would never be any crops. But we can see, in fact, it isn't like this: sometimes there is a result, sometimes there is no result, which means we go back to the impermanent alternative. That, of course, eliminates the possibility of a permanent cause.

Question: Could you explain again why Buddhists don't believe in a creator?

Rinpoche: Some religions and philosophies speak of a creator of the universe. It is believed that "he" makes everything; he makes the world and he also determines the condition of beings. He makes their happiness, he makes their suffering. This creator is believed to be permanent, meaning that the creator is continually present creating the universe for sentient beings to experience. Again if one says he is permanent, everything has to be changeless. Everything has to be as it is once and for all. If this creator-god is permanent, then at all times everything is the same; there is no room for any change. If there is change happening, it means automatically that he is not permanent, so this concept of a permanent creator doesn't stand to reason. It isn't valid.

Question: Christians say that Christ is alive and doesn't that make him permanent?

Rinpoche: Even if one says that Christ is still alive that doesn't mean that he is permanent. Here we are mixing up two different things. When we say permanent, it's not in terms of whether somebody is dead or not dead. It's in terms of whether there is change or no change. That's the level of things when we speak of permanence or impermanence, change or no change.

Question: Can't a permanent creator create change?

Rinpoche: It seems that it's not compatible, because when something is permanent, it's the complete opposite of change. If we say permanence, it means no change. If we consider things in the world, there is constant change. For instance, if we have a cup and it gets a little chip in it, this cup is no longer the same. If it's no longer the same, it has changed. Then it is impermanent. Or if today we are writing, but yesterday we weren't writing, there is a change there. It's impermanent.

In the same way, the world as it is today isn't like the world it was yesterday. There is change. Then if there is change it means there can't be somebody creating the world because it would never change. If there were a permanent creator, things would never change. It is incompatible to have a permanent creator and change in the world.

Question: Surely permanent creation means change by definition. How can you permanently create without changing?

Rinpoche: If the world is created differently every day, then automatically that means there is change. It isn't permanent.

Question: Why does that mean there isn't a force or whatever making that?

Rinpoche: It doesn't mean that it can't be a creator. It means there can't be an eternal creator because there is change.

Question: Millions of beings have visited the earth, and millions of beings will again visit the earth. As far as I know there's not some permanence in that process of change.

Rinpoche: You can't even say that process is permanent, because it will imply that what will come back is exactly the same, like last year's spring is coming back exactly the same and that's impossible. Even if you look at a tree, the tree of this spring might be nine feet in circumference. Next year it might be ten feet, the year after it might be eleven feet. It's not the same tree, it's not the same spring. Something might come back, but it's not the same. You can't say it's the same, so it isn't a permanent thing. It's a different spring that comes.

Question: But the process is repeating itself whatever the spring is doing.

Rinpoche: No. The process is not repeating itself. If the process repeated itself, the spring would have to be exactly the same each year. But it's a different spring each year so it's not a process repeating itself, it's two different things happening.

Question: Are the causes of impermanence, permanent?

Rinpoche: No, even the causes of impermanence are impermanent. If one takes a child, the child is impermanent and his mother is impermanent so the cause is impermanent and the result is impermanent.

Question: The *dharmakaya* is a kind of permanence and *sambhogakaya* and nirmanakaya are based on the dharmakaya, so in other words the nirmanakaya is effortless and it doesn't matter. It's produced by the dharmakaya, more or less, while it's supposed to be permanent. And it's always different.

Rinpoche: At the moment we are speaking of impermanence, to refute the idea of a real permanence, a permanence that is of things as being substantial and substantially real. It is to refute the belief in real, solid existence. When we speak of the dharmakaya being permanent, it is in the sense that the emptiness of the dharmakaya is there all the time. It isn't in the sense of the dharmakaya being a solid, real, substantial thing.

Question: I think that God refers to the dharmakaya, not to the rule of the gods as you translated. The God of the Catholics can refer to the dharmakaya.

Rinpoche: If one can see the god, whether it is Christian or another view, as being something that is not substantially real. If one conceives him as being emptiness, then of course it's permanent. But if one conceives of him as being a real substantial thing, then it is impermanent.

Chapter 5

The Nine Stages of Placing the Mind

In our study of the system of meditation of the Middle-way, we saw that the first step is to develop and practice compassion. The second step is to develop bodhichitta to achieve enlightenment for the sake of all beings. The third step is to develop knowledge and understanding in its highest form, prajna. This is done through study, reflection, and finally through meditation. We saw that the first two steps of study and reflection are intended to help us develop a strong conviction of the way things really are, not simply as they appear. Once we have acquired that certainty, we learn how to rest the mind within this. So through study we gain certainty and through reflection that certainty becomes very clear and integrated. Once we have this very clear conviction, we learn how to immerse our mind in this emptiness. This is what we will consider today. There are nine different ways in which we can do this.

The Nine Stages of Placing the Mind

There are nine ways in which one can make the mind rest within the conviction that things are inherently empty. The first stage is called "placing" and this is simply placing the mind. First there has to be the conviction concerning the nature of phenomena; that their actual nature is empty beyond all extremes, and beyond all conceptual fabrications, at the same time understanding that this emptiness isn't a blankness, a void nothing, but has a presence of great clarity and lucidity. So it's the conviction of the nature of phenomena according to the Middle-way. The first step consists of letting the mind remain within this clear conviction, placing the mind on this without the interference of thoughts.

The second stage is called "continuous resting." At first we may be able to rest our mind within that conviction for only a short instant. The second step is learning to do this for a little longer, so the meditation can go on a little longer.

Once we are able to prolong the meditation a little, then the next thing that will happen is that thoughts will arise for more than just a very short instant. These thoughts will take different forms, being thoughts of the past, thoughts of the future, and thoughts of the present. Once we fall under the influence of these thoughts, we forget the continuity of our conviction by being engaged in the thread of our desire, and our concentration will dissolve. Our mind will be following the thoughts and we will have forgotten the object of our meditation.

The third stage of the meditation is to reestablish our placement. We have to put the mind back into a state of immersion. This is the point where we realize, "Well, that thought has come. I've forgotten what I was doing in the first place." This is the point where we acknowledge the presence of the thought. We recognize it as such, but at the same time, we don't make a very strong discrimination about the thoughts by clinging to the thoughts themselves. We don't think, "This is a good thought," or "That is a bad thought. Now my meditation has gone down the drain." We don't make this kind of distinction. We just relax, let go of the thought, and then go back into that first immersion by placing the mind in the certainty that we had to begin with.

The fourth stage of the meditation is called "real immersion" or "even closer immersion." It is still the same basic idea as in the beginning, but it is stronger. When we are looking at the essence of mind, thoughts manifest. Then sometimes we may feel that thoughts are quite good things, that they are rather interesting. Other times we feel that thoughts are a source of problems, because we're continually thinking, "This is no good. I'm not happy like this. I need this. I want that." Under the influence of all these different kinds of thoughts our mind will feel splintered, it won't be very peaceful, and it will generate discomfort, problems, and difficulties. Now in this fourth stage of the meditation the right thing to do is just to drop the thought altogether; just leave it. We're not trying to stop the thought forcibly, but we're trying to let go of it. If we do that, the distraction will dissolve automatically. It will disappear and in its place will be a feeling of relief, of joy, happiness, relaxation, and peace. The point of this fourth stage is to immerse ourselves once again within the peaceful feeling that arises once we have been able to let go of thoughts. So if we let go of the thoughts, a very peaceful, relaxed and pleasant feeling will result.

The fifth stage is called "training the mind" or "taming the mind." When we are not meditating, such as taking a break or doing something else, the point of this fifth step is to remember very clearly all the goodness of meditation, remembering that meditation brings us great joy, great relaxation, and great peace and happiness in the short term. In the long term, meditation can eliminate all negativity and can help us find true peace which brings the end of suffering. So we should remain mindful of these qualities of meditation and also remember the feelings of happiness, peace, and relaxation that we experience in meditation. If we can remain mindful of this while in post-meditation, then we will develop more and more appreciation of what meditation is, so that we can immerse ourselves in the meditation very easily and naturally. If we can do this, then automatically the meditation becomes easier, and the obstacles in the form of thoughts will vanish more easily. So the point of being aware of the good qualities and the positive feelings of the meditation is to be so appreciative of meditation that we are easily inclined to practice. It makes the meditation easier and more effective.

The sixth stage of the meditation is called "pacifying," or making peaceful. The content of this sixth step is very similar to the previous one of taming the mind. The point is to make the mind more workable through appreciating the good qualities of meditation, so that we can meditate more easily. The goal is the same, but it is achieved in a different way. Pacifying is achieved through being aware of the devastating effects of thoughts and distractions. It is to realize that while we are not meditating and we fall under the influence of thoughts, our mind will be disturbed and agitated. Once our mind is agitated, we are unable to function properly and are dominated by all sorts of negative states. In the longer term, if our mind is very agitated, we won't be able to meditate properly. We won't be able to eliminate our negative aspects and in the end won't be able to achieve Buddhahood. The sixth stage is a reflection on all the negative effects of thoughts and distractions. This reflection will bring our mind to a point where it is not willing to become involved with thoughts, to generate thoughts, or to follow thoughts. In this sense the sixth stage achieves the same effect as the previous step but through different techniques.

The seventh stage is called "completely pacifying" or making really peaceful. It's the same Tibetan word for "pacifying" as used before but it's one step further. The first six stages were designed mainly to increase the stability of mind. They were steps to avoid distraction, to avoid falling under the influence of thoughts, and to provide stability and tranquillity of mind both during and after meditation. However, there is a danger that when we are always thinking in terms of stabilizing the mind or concentrating, we might go too far by concentrating too hard. The result of this over-concentration is that the mind becomes quite unclear and drowsy. It's a form of heaviness of the mind, much the same feeling we get when we are very tired. When this heaviness of mind grows deeper, we fall asleep. This comes from putting too much effort on concentrating the mind. The way to eliminate this excessive tension, both physical and mental, is to take a break in the meditation.

The eighth and ninth stages of meditation correspond to what we do or do not do in reaction to the faults that may occur in meditation. We said before that there are two basic mistakes that may occur in meditation: having too much agitation of the mind with too many thoughts, or mental dullness, which in the end leads to sleep. The first way to deal with these two conditions is to realize that we are not making enough effort to be aware of what is going on in our meditation. We are not aware of what defects are occurring in our meditation so we do not try hard enough to get rid of those defects and improve the meditation. Basically, there is a lack of effort and the remedy to this is to refocus, to concentrate in order to find out what the defects in our meditation are. If we find our meditation is good, then we just remain within this and let it develop. But if we find that there is a defect in our meditation, we try to use the remedy to correct.

We may not be making enough effort in our meditation and this causes problems. There is also the possibility of doing too much. For example, we may come to a point in meditation where our mind is no longer very agitated or distracted or in a state of torpor. We have reached a point where our mind is fairly stable and relaxed. At this point if we interfere with the mind, trying to modify the meditation, it's a mistake. We have to modify our meditation only when it's needed. But once the mind has found its state of concentration, we must leave it in its own balance without interfering. It's like a bowl of muddy water, if you just put the bowl down for a little while, the mud in the water will simply settle. But if you keep on moving the container about, the water will never settle. In the same way, we have to refocus the mind when there are defects in the meditation such as when it's too agitated or too drowsy. But once the mind regains its own balance, then we must just let it stay in its own balance without interfering any more. That is why this ninth stage is called "resting within the balance of mind."

Applying the Nine Stages of Meditation

How are we to apply these nine stages of meditation? We have to go through each one as a progression, beginning with the first stage of immersing the mind within the conviction that we have acquired the understanding of the nature of things. So we have this basic certainty and then we learn how to put our mind within this for a brief moment. We do this many times until it becomes quite familiar. Once we are familiar with this stage, we can go on to the second stage which is prolonging this experience by increasing the time during which we let the mind rest within the basic certainty that we have concerning the nature of things.

The third stage concerns what to do once thoughts appear in our meditation. In this stage we place the mind back into its immersion, trying to make our meditation more stable. This will be achieved through the fourth stage which is to completely immerse the mind. In this fourth stage we will also have to use some effort when we are in post-meditation. We work on post-meditation particularly in the five and six stages which are taming and pacifying the mind.

In the fifth and sixth stages we learn how to let go of thoughts and gain more peace and also to become appreciative of the qualities of meditation, so that meditation automatically becomes easier. Then we use the seventh stage, which enables us to eliminate the problems of agitation or torpor when we encounter them in our meditation. So we will have to learn how to concentrate, how to focus more sharply when it is needed. Then in the last two stages we finally learn how not to interfere when the mind is in the right state of balance and we stay within that balance of the mind.

If we use all these nine stages, our meditation will progress without any major problem. As said before, there are two kinds of meditation: analytical meditation and placement meditation. Here we are speaking mostly in terms of analytical meditation because this is a meditation that can become very stable. Analytical meditation is the traditional way of meditation of the sutras which doesn't leave any room for mistakes or misunderstanding. There is no risk of analytical meditation falling into what is called "stupid meditation." With placement meditation we may be able to see the nature of mind directly from time to time; we may have a flash of the nature of mind. But there is also a risk that in placement meditation we won't really see anything and will fall into a very stupid, blank state, which isn't very productive. So in the process described here, we begin with study in order to understand what the path is all about. Then we reflect on the basis of this study, developing enough certainty concerning the nature of phenomena. Once we have this certainty, we learn how to immerse ourselves within that certainty. If we follow this method of meditation, we can never fall into "stupid meditation."

Meditation of Direct Examination of Mind

In connection with meditation, there are two different ways to integrate one's meditation with the path. One is to integrate logical reasoning with one's path. Once one has gained certainty about the nature of phenomena through logical examination, then one keeps this as one's object of meditation and immerses oneself in it again and again until it becomes very clear and continues progressing.

The other aspect is to integrate direct understanding with the path, as is used in *vajrayana* meditation. This meditation, called placement meditation, or "looking directly at mind," is not a Middle-way technique. One looks directly at the nature of mind, one recognizes one's mind, which is the very expression of the ultimate nature of all phenomena. This is used as one's main practice and is, in fact, the highest aspect of meditation. The first method, of using logical understanding, is very useful because it makes one's meditation very stable. This path is outlined in all the sutra paths of meditation, including the Middle-way meditation. One shouldn't think that it is an inferior way, because it is indeed extremely useful, making the mind very stable.

On the other hand, the vajrayana technique of direct understanding of mind is very beneficial because it makes it possible to gain understanding very quickly. This is called the short path. Actually the best meditation is a combination of both these methods: from time to time using the short path technique of direct understanding and then using the Middle-way technique of inferential understanding. If one uses both, it is possible to have a very stable mind and to progress very rapidly on the path.

The techniques that I personally used for meditation in the vajrayana were mostly based on *yidam meditation*, using visualization on a deity.[13] This technique improves one's capacity for meditation. Also the vajrayana method of meditation can be based on one's devotion in the practice of *guru yoga meditation,* in which one develops devotion towards one's guru. This is another way to progress in meditation.

Gathering Virtue

In addition to the meditative practices outlined according to the Middle-way, there are also activities we can do to progress more quickly in our meditation. These are basically acting in a positive way and gathering virtue. Gathering virtue includes activities such as making offerings and prayers to the *three jewels*, in the form of the representations of the Buddha's body, speech, mind, and so on. It also involves meditation on compassion towards all beings, and once the feeling of compassion is developed, trying to do whatever one can in order to help and protect other beings.

The accumulation of virtue actually covers all of the aspects of the transcendental perfections or *paramitas*. It covers generosity, such as giving in whatever way you can, either giving protection from fear, giving material things, or teaching the Dharma. It also involves practicing moral discipline by either taking all the monastic vows, or taking the precepts for lay people.[14] It doesn't necessarily mean taking them for life; they can be taken for just a month or even for a few days. What is important is a promise to act in a certain positive way and to avoid acting in a negative way for that given amount of time.

Another way to gather virtue in Middle-way meditation is to develop patience in general by trying to eliminate all aspects of negativity, but eliminating anger in particular. Every day we can make a little effort towards diminishing anger. We might decide to set a certain amount of time every day during which we will make a particular effort not to get angry. Also we can try to think of all the harm and the danger of anger, so that we are quite convinced of anger's negative results. If we do so, we will find that there is a natural decrease of anger, just by being aware of its destructiveness. That is another way of developing our virtue through the practice of patience. Then we can practice diligence and meditation and the understanding which is developed by all of these practices.

In addition to the actual technique of meditation, if we really want meditation to develop within us, we will also have to engage in forms of accumulation of virtue, because this is what will develop a naturally peaceful mind, which helps the development of meditation.

Chapter 6

The Obstacles to Meditation and their Remedies

In our study of meditation of the Middle-way, we saw that the preparation for the actual meditation consists of the meditation on compassion and the intention to develop bodhichitta within oneself. The actual practice could be called either the development of prajna or the development of the understanding of emptiness. Prajna is developed in three ways; first through study, then through contemplation, and finally through meditation.

In the last chapter, we saw that we are trying to develop the certainty of the emptiness of phenomena that has been acquired through study and reflection. We also try to stabilize the mind, which is achieved through nine stages. At the end of this path we reach the point where if there are faults in the meditation, we have to concentrate more. But if the mind is balanced, then we just rest in the balanced state.

What are the faults in meditation and how can we remove them? And if there are good qualities in the meditation, how can we increase them? We can answer these questions by describing six main obstacles that can disturb our meditation and the eight different techniques that we can use to overcome these six obstacles.

The Six Obstacles to Meditation

The first obstacle we encounter in meditation is laziness. The whole point of meditation is to develop the habit of a meditative state of mind. But we have been in conditioned existence (Skt. *samsara*) for so long that we have formed very bad habits. It is quite difficult to reverse these habits overnight; in fact, it takes quite a bit of effort to overcome these bad habits and to establish positive ones. If we fall under the influence of laziness, it will be quite difficult for us to meditate because we won't feel like meditating. We will say, "Well, I don't have time to meditate." Even if there is the time we may feel, "I won't do it today, but I'll do it tomorrow." If we actually get the chance to meditate, we think, "I don't feel like it now, it's not quite the right time." Even if we come to the point where we are actually going to meditate, we won't feel happy at all about it. We won't feel that it is something we enjoy doing. This is all due to the problem of laziness. Laziness is what stops us from wanting to meditate and that is why we don't even begin to meditate.

Even if we come to the point where we actually start meditating, laziness will stop us from following through. Instead of having a nice, long session, we will have a very short one. While we are meditating, because we are not very interested in meditating, our meditation will not be very clear. We will be following all sorts of chains of thoughts, and our meditation will be one of obstacles. Instead of having a few good qualities and a few obstacles, it will be overridden with many obstacles. This is all due to the problem of laziness because we are not really interested in meditating. We don't really want to meditate.

Laziness in general is an obstacle in whatever you want to do. If you have a goal that you have chosen for yourself and you have fallen prey to laziness, this, of course, will be a great obstacle to the realization of that goal. This is true in general matters and it is also very true in the spiritual sense. Laziness is a strong stumbling block to the birth of true meditation.

The second main obstacle that may arise in meditation is forgetfulness, specifically, when one forgets the object of meditation. This is due to a lack of mindfulness. This forgetfulness means that one has either forgotten what the qualities of the meditation are or the instructions on the meditation. Or one forgets how one is supposed to meditate, what the point of the meditation is, or what the benefit of the meditation is. Once one forgets these, the meditation cannot be correct anymore, whereas if one can keep these in mind, then one's meditation will become clearer and clearer.

Forgetfulness can take two forms. One form is that you have forgotten all about the instructions, both the words and the meaning.

The other form is that you may still remember the words, but you don't remember to apply the instructions, so you receive the instructions from your teacher, but you forget all about applying them to your meditation. The result of this forgetfulness is that you are deprived of the tools of the methods that will help you to really meditate.

These first two obstacles, that of laziness and that of forgetting the meditation instructions, constitute an obstacle to starting the practice of meditation. These two obstacles stop us from actually beginning the meditation. The third and fourth obstacles, those of drowsiness and agitation, arise in the course of meditation. They won't stop us from beginning the meditation, but once we have begun, they won't allow it to become clear and stable.

The third obstacle of drowsiness prevents the meditation from being clear. This lack of clarity of mind can take many different forms. The mildest form is drowsiness, when our mind just begins to be a little unclear. When this becomes greater, it becomes lethargy, in which we feel very heavy and sleepy. Then, if this carries on, it leads to sleep, causing meditation to fail. This obstacle begins at the moment when drowsiness sets in and our meditation becomes unclear. So this is an obstacle to clarity in meditation.

The fourth obstacle is agitation. Literally, this word in Tibetan means "wildness" indicating that we can't really do anything with our mind anymore. We can't control it and the mind goes wild in the sense that it is constantly churning up all sorts of thoughts. We may start thinking about the past or future plans or what's going on just now. Even though we may want to make the mind a little bit more stable, we can't do it and our mind goes off into another chain of thoughts, becoming involved with thoughts of anger, jealousy, desire, or ordinary things. Once we get into this state of mental agitation, it's very difficult to regain clarity. We just follow one thought after another, making this an obstacle to stability.

The fifth obstacle to the development of the meditation is called "lack of effort." For meditation to progress we have to eliminate whatever faults are in the meditation, and conversely, we have to try to develop whatever positive aspects are there. All this requires a certain amount of effort. First we examine the quality of our meditation to actually see if anything is wrong. Once we discover that something is wrong, we have to identify exactly what is wrong. Is it caused by laziness, forgetfulness, drowsiness, or agitation? After identifying the problem, we have to apply more effort to eliminate the problem, so we will have to try to apply the corresponding remedy for any of the obstacles identified. But if there is no effort to do this, then all the faults will continue in the meditation and the quality of the meditation will not increase, making an obstacle to the meditation.

The sixth obstacle is called "excessive effort." This occurs when we are constantly looking and checking our meditation; thinking something is going wrong and always trying to modify it. Instead, we should check from time to time to see if there is the risk of a mistake, and if there is no mistake, there is nothing to do. There's no reason to interfere and try to change things, because the point of meditation is to let the mind be, to become completely relaxed. This is possible only when the mind is not under the influence of any of these defects. So when the mind is in this very relaxed and peaceful state, we must just let it be without disturbing the balance of the mind.

In this way the six main problems encountered in meditation are described, the first two being an obstacle to the beginning of the meditation, the next two being an obstacle to the actual meditation itself, and the last two being an obstacle to its progress. Of course, we could point out many more mistakes and problems encountered in meditation, but really all of these are included within the six main obstacles. We should study these six main obstacles so that when we encounter them in meditation, we can identify them. Once we have identified the problem, we know how to remedy it. If we don't find any of these obstacles in the meditation, we can just let our mind be very relaxed. However, if we don't know these six obstacles and how to eliminate them, then it won't be possible to achieve much in meditation because our meditation will not be able to develop become clear.

Eight Remedies to Meditation

After having examined the six obstacles, we will look at the eight remedies to these problems.

There are four remedies to the first obstacle of laziness: appreciation, aspiration, diligence, and workability. Appreciation, the first remedy, is that whatever object you consider, you realize its qualities, you realize it is a good thing, and you turn towards it with interest and liking. This appreciation is applied to meditation because this is what will make you want to practice. Whereas if you do not practice, your mind will become less and less workable and produce more and more troubles and suffering. But meditation that trains the mind will make it become very smooth, very peaceful, very relaxed.

Meditation will be of benefit to you and others as well. Once the mind is very peaceful, you won't have so many difficulties, suffering, or unhappiness. This will also have very good effects for others, insofar as once you are more peaceful and self-controlled, you won't have so many outbreaks of anger, desire, or pride. You become a real friend to others. Appreciation is a matter of developing a real feeling of trust and confidence in the qualities of meditation and thus appreciation will act as an antidote to laziness.

The second antidote is aspiration, which in Tibetan also means "interest." When you have this basic appreciation for meditation, you really want to practice even though you know your meditation contains many defects. Once you are aware of its goodness, you really want to develop this within you. You develop a feeling you must meditate and you won't forget doing it. You have an intense desire to meditate. This aspiration is the second antidote to laziness.

Through appreciation we come to really know the wonderful qualities of meditation and this leads us to the second antidote, the wish to actually meditate. Once we have the appreciation for meditation and the will to meditate, automatically we will have the necessary diligence to do the meditation. We won't have to force ourselves. It's simply because we want to do it so much, that we will do it. Through this inspired diligence, we won't wait a long time before we begin. Once we actually meditate, we will be able to go on for quite a while with great enthusiasm. Through the will to meditate, diligence will arise automatically, so that every day we will be able to meditate for longer and longer times. Diligence constitutes the third antidote to laziness.

Once there is this very enthusiastic, very joyful diligence in the practice of meditation, the mind will automatically become workable, which is the fourth antidote, the workability of the mind. When the mind is rough and undisciplined, it is very hard to make it do anything. We might think "Now I want to think in this way" or "I want to do this," but we can't get our mind to do it because our mind is very unmanageable. We can't get it to work the way we want. Once our mind is well-trained, we can do this very easily. But before it is well-trained, the mind is mixed up and it will hesitate thinking, "Maybe it's good to do, but I can't actually do it." This way we won't be able to work on our mind and this constitutes an obstacle in our meditation. But as soon as there is appreciation of meditation, diligence will arise automatically and very joyfully. Then the mind will just do whatever is required and it will do it very clearly for a long time.

A good example of this occurred when Marpa was speaking to Milarepa after Milarepa had been meditating for eleven months at one sitting. Marpa said, "Well, eleven months of meditation like this may be a bit too much, because your mind and your body may get tired, and consequently your meditation won't be very clear. So perhaps you should take a little rest." Milarepa replied, "I don't think there is any rest apart from what I've been doing." Meaning he couldn't conceive that what he had been doing wasn't a form of rest. His wish to practice and his joy in the practice were so great that he never felt any tiredness, any need to rest, and he felt there was no better rest than his practice of meditation. The reason why Milarepa could see his practice as relaxation was that his mind was so perfectly workable, having the presence of the first three factors— the appreciation, the wish to meditate, and diligence. When all these three factors are present, laziness will automatically vanish.

Among the eight remedies, the first four remedies are antidotes for laziness, with laziness being the first of the six obstacles. The remedy for the second obstacle of forgetfulness is mindfulness. Mindfulness means that one remains very attentive to what one is doing, to the benefits of good meditation, and to the faults of improper meditation. One doesn't forget this, but keeps it continuously in mind.

The remedy for the third and fourth obstacles of drowsiness and agitation is the sixth remedy of awareness. This means that one is fully aware of what is going on in the mind while meditating, so that if there are many thoughts, one knows it. One doesn't just follow them and become carried away, but one is completely aware of what's going on. If there is drowsiness or agitation in meditation, one knows it's there. Once one is aware of the obstacle, one can do what is required to eliminate it. It's being clearly aware of what is going on in one's mind all the time during meditation. This is the remedy to both drowsiness and agitation.

The fifth and sixth obstacles are a lack of effort and excess of effort, respectively. The seventh remedy is attentiveness, which is used to counteract the lack of effort. Attentiveness is producing more effort in the meditation. The eighth remedy is applied to the excess of effort. This is a neutral state of mind, whereby the mind remains very relaxed, very peaceful, without interference.

So these eight antidotes to the six obstacles are the way to develop our meditation and clarity. At first we have to recognize the six obstacles, and then we have to use the eight remedies to get rid of them. These obstacles and their remedies were not simply the creation of scholars of the Middle-way, but rather they were the fruition of realized persons who were both scholars and practitioners. They practiced what was taught in the sutras of the Buddha, and while they were practicing, they encountered the normal problems that anybody who practices encounters. When they had these difficulties, they tried to find out what were the best ways to overcome the problems. On the basis of their experiences and on the basis the Buddha's teachings in the sutras, they put together this system of meditative techniques and remedies. These obstacles and their remedies were the natural outcome of the experience of these great beings.

The best thing for us to do is to use these tools in our practice. In the same way that the great adepts practiced, we will be able to do the same using the fruits of their experience. These instructions shouldn't be the object of intellectual speculation, but an object of our own experience. If we just use these obstacles for speculation, then they won't be of very much benefit and might even be misleading. But if we really apply them to our own practice, they will be very beneficial to us.

We can give an example. If someone asked an intelligent person who has never been to Samye Ling (the Dharma center where

Rinpoche was giving the teaching), "What do you have to do to go to Samye Ling? What do you have to take with you?" That person won't be able to give good advice because he has never experienced staying at Samye Ling. But if that person asked the same question of someone who has lived in Samye Ling, then this person will say, "Well, don't take cool clothes with you because it's a place with a really cold climate. The weather is really bad, so take warm and useful things." Then when this newcomer arrives in Samye Ling, he'll think, "That person was really right. It's just like that." He will realize that the advice that was given was extremely useful because now he has brought the right things. So advice given from someone's experience turns out to be very useful. In the same way, what these great scholars and realized beings have said about meditation came out of their own experience. Once we try to apply it to ourselves, we will see that what they said is very relevant and completely true. When we meditate, we are going to encounter various problems and when we encounter these problems, we will be able to use the remedies that they have discovered. So we should always keep these obstacles and remedies in mind and not forget to apply them in our practice.

Chapter 7

Tranquillity Meditation in the Middle-way

Developing the Right Attitude

Any real benefit coming from Dharma practice depends entirely on our own mind and our own motivation. It doesn't depend on anything or anybody else. To begin with, we have to have a really strong wish to practice the Dharma. But if we don't have a real wish to practice, still having doubts as to how it might be useful or how much we might be able to achieve, then, of course, we won't be able to achieve very much. Apart from our spiritual friend who might advise us in the right way of behaving, no one else can really make us change this attitude.

Of course it's very rare that someone will be able to have a very pure motivation from the start and spontaneously think that he or she wants to achieve enlightenment for the sake of all beings. How can we try to develop that way of thinking? We can think about the way the Buddha showed this to us very clearly and that having bodhichitta is the most beneficial attitude to hold. We can also rely on the words of the Buddha and other great realized individuals to understand the need for such pure motivation and its very beneficial nature. Once we are aware of this and try to keep this motivation in mind, we will have to try again and again to generate very pure motivation. By doing this repeatedly, it will become much easier because we will have a very strong conviction of the usefulness of the attitude of bodhichitta and in the end it will arise automatically without the need for any great effort. This is why we must continuously try to think that the very reason to do what we are doing is to become a buddha for the sake of all beings. The reason we receive teachings is so that we can achieve this fruition properly and quickly.

Shantideva explained that if one wants to achieve anything, whether we are speaking in terms of ultimate realization or proper meditation, the first prerequisite is that the mind be disposed in the proper way. If the mind is right, then everything else will be achieved effortlessly. But if the attitude is wrong, everything else will go wrong as well. The example that Shantideva used to illustrate this was to compare the mind to a white elephant that has gone berserk. An elephant is a strong animal and if it goes mad, it becomes extremely dangerous. Likewise, the mind is also tremendously powerful. It might not seem so at first because the mind appears to not really be doing anything. But think how the atom bomb that has created so much fear and apprehension in so many individuals in the world was only a thought in the mind of some scientists. But because this thought was developed into something, it became this terrible, fearful weapon that can destroy the whole world. So the mind is very much like a wild elephant. If we let the elephant just run wild, it will spread havoc, destroying things. It will be most dangerous; it cannot do anything right, it can only do things wrong. But if we can control the elephant, there won't be any problems. If we train the elephant, we can use its strength for valuable work. In the same way, the mind is our own mind and since it is our mind, it must be quite easy to regain control over it. If we can do this, we won't have to worry about any suffering and we will find happiness. This is why Shantideva says in *A Guide to the Bodhisattva's Way of Life* that "we must tie the wild elephant of the mind to the post of Dharma."

We saw that the atom bomb, the cause of so much fear, was contained within the intention in someone's mind. In the same way, everything we experience in conditioned existence—all our fears, all our suffering—are rooted in the mind, in our way of thinking. The way to find liberation from all this also is rooted in a way of thinking that we can generate within ourselves. So we have to train the mind to think in the proper way, otherwise we fall into a constant cycle of difficulties, sorrows, and suffering. But if we can train the mind, we will be able to experience all the forms of goodness and happiness because all of this comes from our mind. So here the priority is not how we should relate to outer things, but how to control our own mind.

There are many different ways that we can train the mind. We saw previously that in terms of relative truth, we can use development of compassion. In the system of the Middle-way meditation, we can use the meditation on the basis of the certainty developed through reflective contemplation.

The Four Stages of Tranquillity Meditation

There are two fundamental kinds of meditation in the Middle-way. These are tranquillity meditation (Skt. *shamatha*) and insight meditation (Skt. *vipashyana*). Tranquillity meditation is making the mind remain in a state of tranquillity without allowing it to fall prey to thoughts and negative factors that could disturb it. Insight meditation is seeing very clearly and very vividly the ultimate nature of phenomena. Tranquillity meditation and insight meditation are practiced at all levels of meditation from the beginner up to achieving Buddhahood itself.

Tranquillity and insight meditation can be described in four stages. The first stage is called "one-pointedness," which occurs when the beginner needs to develop very strong mental concentration. The second stage is called "no complication" which occurs when one is learning to experience the true state of phenomena directly as being free from all the complications that are created by our thoughts, concepts, and ideas. The third stage is called "one-taste" which occurs when one experiences all things as having basically the same flavor or essence within the ultimate nature; everything is the same within that nature; so we say everything tastes the same. Finally, the last stage is called "no-meditation" because there is nothing more to do. One is just immersed within the ultimate nature of things and therefore one doesn't have to do any separate meditation. So these are the four levels of practice that should be practiced gradually, one after the other. It's very much like the idea of a ladder or staircase. If one wants to go upstairs, one has to take one step after the other. One can't jump onto the higher steps before you have used the lower steps, so one step gradually leads to the next step.

Let us consider the first stage of meditation of one-pointedness in more detail. This stage is a matter of developing concentration and there are many different ways to achieve this. First there is a physical condition, which is to put one's body in the seven-pointed meditation posture called the Vairocana posture.[15] Then there are different ways to develop the mind, different ways of developing concentration.[16] One can use a support or use no support for this development of concentration. A support can be an external or an inner support. An external support may be an impure one, such as a little stone or piece of wood. A pure external support could be something like a statue of the Buddha to represent the Buddha's pure body, or it could be a Tibetan letter to represent the Buddha's pure speech, or it could be a little sphere (Skt. *bindu*) to represent the Buddha's pure mind.

There are also inner supports, the main one being concentrating on our breathing during meditation. One can either count or follow the breath. There are many different techniques of breathing meditation. This is what is called basic "sitting meditation" and is fairly easy to follow. If one follows the instructions, one can go through them and experience them and develop concentration.

After we have trained our mind using an external or internal support, we can begin meditating without support. The first step is to make a very strong resolution that we are going to meditate. We must first put ourselves in the right frame of mind. If we decide to meditate for a month, then we think during that month, "Now I'm not going to spend time thinking or planning or being involved with ideas of my work or activities. I'm not going to spend my time talking or doing all sorts of ordinary things." This is very important, because if we constantly have thoughts of our work or activities, we won't be able to meditate properly, because all these different thoughts will be a source of agitation, creating an obstacle to our concentration. Whether we decide to spend ten minutes, or an hour, or a week in meditation, before we begin there must be an understanding that during this meditation time we are not going to do or think about anything else. When we finish with the meditation, then we can go back to our chores and occupation and do whatever we have to do. But while we are meditating, we must be very relaxed and free from our usual concerns. So when we begin our meditation, it's essential to think, "Now I'm going to meditate. I'm not going to think of my work. I'm not going to think about my occupation. I'm not going to make plans about this or that. I'm not going to be concerned about any of these things." What we do with our body is that we don't become involved with any activity. Then we should not be involved in talking because if we start talking, our speech will go on and on until our mind is completely disturbed. Finally with our mind, we must decide to apply ourselves completely to the improvement of concentration, however long or short it is. We must not become involved with plans or thinking how we can improve our situation or how we can get rid of problems. Just give up all those ideas of planning and arranging completely and resolve that we are not going to be bothered with any of those things. We will just devote ourselves to trying to develop more concentration. Once we have put our mind in the right frame of mind, we will be able to meditate properly. This is because there will be what is called physical, verbal, and mental solitude.

When we meditate, we also have to avoid thinking in terms of the past, present, and future. While meditating, we often have thoughts of what happened yesterday or a few minutes ago or even a few years ago. We will remember when we had very nice experiences or when something very nasty and painful happened to us. But in fact all these thoughts are pointless, since whatever happened previously is now finished. If we suffered at one point, that particular suffering is no longer here, it is gone. Also any happy situation is no longer here, it is finished. That is the very nature of the past, it doesn't come back. It's like a dead person, so there's no point thinking of the past, because the past is gone; it's irrelevant.

We also have thoughts of the future, by making plans, thinking what we will do tomorrow or next month or next year. We begin thinking, "I'm going to do this or that" or "I'm going to say this or that" but all of this isn't useful, because all we are doing is raising a lot of thoughts with no guarantee that these thoughts are going to have any reality later on.

There is a story that is used as an example in instructions for meditation. There was a man who was very, very poor. One day through hard work he managed to earn a sack of grain. He was very happy with it, so at night he hung the sack above his head. Before going to sleep, he considered what had happened to him. He was very happy with his sack of grain. He thought, "Now I'm going to establish myself nicely in this world. Now I've got this grain, I think I'm going to get married, and once I've gotten married I want to have a child." Then he began considering what name to give the child, and the moon was starting to rise outside, so he thought, "I'm going to call the child Famous Moon," and at that point, the rope that was holding the sack broke and it fell on his head and killed him. This story shows that there is no need to make plans because our plans don't always come true. In the instructions of meditation, it says, "Do not anticipate."[17] There's no point because the future is most likely not going to be what you anticipate. When you begin to meditate, think that you are not going to anticipate the future and just stay in the meditation.

If we must not follow thoughts of past and future, what about the present? The present seems a rather long time especially when we think in terms of today or this month or this year. However, with closer inspection, the present is only a very, very brief moment. It actually lasts only the very instant of a thought. What we have to do in the meditation is be within this very instant of thought and just let the mind be within that present moment. Thoughts are likely to go in all directions and then we will find it very difficult to stop them, because we can't really control them. But controlling thoughts isn't the point of the meditation; it is to just look directly at the thoughts and just relax within the thought itself so that it vanishes. There is no such thing as a solid thought once you look at it and relax within it. It just goes away automatically like clouds in the sky.

When we meditate, we shouldn't think that meditation means to force our mind in a stringent way. Meditation is not a straitjacket for the mind, but it's a matter of relaxing as much as we can and to ease ourselves within the thoughts at that particular instant of mind. Sometimes we may have a good thought, but there is no need to think, "Oh, that's a really good thought, I must keep that one, I must not let it go." The moment we recognize that thought, we just let our mind rest within it, and the thought will automatically vanish. Then sometimes we may have nasty thoughts and may think, "Oh, I'm really terrible, look at what I'm thinking, it's really awful, I must get rid of that negative thought." But again there's no need to think in that way, we just relax within the thought and it will disappear completely spontaneously. Concerning the present it is said, "Do not change anything with regard to the present mind, just rest within it."

At first it may seem that the thoughts are quite real, quite solid, and permanent and we can't stop them. This is because we have not really examined our mind. In fact, we are completely misinformed about what is going on in our mind. We are under the illusion of mistaking what is an absence of thought for an actual thought. If we start looking into our mind, we won't find any such thing as a thought. Where does the thought come from? Where does it go? The thought doesn't have a beginning and it doesn't have an end. However, where there is no thought, we think there are thoughts. But, in fact, within the actual nature of the mind, there are no thoughts. That is the very reason why there is no need for us to try to stop or to follow thoughts, because there are no such things as thoughts. By nature the mind is completely peaceful and relaxed, and if we can just allow it to be as it is, there is no question of fighting the thoughts and getting rid of them. It is a matter of recognizing that thoughts are not a result of mistakes we made in meditation. We are realizing and beginning to experience the mind within its natural state.[18]

Chart 2

*The Nine Levels of Stability of Meditation**

1. Resting the mind
   (One places one's mind on an object for a brief duration.)

2. Resting the mind longer
   (One places one's mind on an object and it wanders and then one places it back again on the object.)

3. Continuously resettling the mind
   (One keeps placing one's mind, but there are still thoughts such as "this is important" or "I like this" which prevent complete placement.)

4. Intensely settled mind
   (The mind appears to be vast and the thoughts appear only as small intrusions on this vast space.)

5. Taming the mind
   (One feels joy, enthusiasm, and relaxation in one's meditation.)

6. Pacification of the mind
   (The mind appears tame, but it still wanders because we are still attached to these wanderings.)

7. Complete pacification of the mind
   (Whenever a distraction appears in the mind, one immediately applies the right antidote.)

8. One-pointed mind
   (One can place the mind almost completely, but it still requires some exertion.)

9. Resting in equanimity
   (Mind rests simply and naturally in its own nature.)

*These nine ways were first given in the *Ornament of Clear Realization* of Maitreya.

Chapter 8

Cutting Through Thoughts

Our mind is the source of all our happiness and all our suffering. If we can control our mind, if we are the master of our mind, we will have the source of our happiness and we won't need to rely on any outer objects to make us happy. If, on the other hand, we don't control our mind, we will always fall prey to thoughts, to negativity, and no matter how many outer pleasures we possess, we will never be able to enjoy them. Without control of our mind we won't be able to fulfill our wishes, because within us there won't be the real cause of satisfaction, and again we will end up suffering. That is why the very first teaching of the Buddha was the importance of learning how to control, how to tame, how to train our mind. This is because with great insight and compassion the Buddha saw that an untrained mind was the primary cause of all beings' suffering and happiness.

The Buddha did not say that we must stop looking for happiness and must continue suffering. It is the universal wish of all beings, wherever they are, whoever they are, to be happy and not to suffer. However they are not able to achieve this because they don't know the way to find happiness and avoid suffering. So what the Buddha did was simply to show how we could achieve happiness and how we could eliminate suffering.

When the Buddha showed the means to achieve happiness, it wasn't in the form of terrible austerities and asceticism. He showed that all happiness can be achieved through one thing: knowing one's mind and eliminating ignorance; this is the source of all happiness and the key to ending all suffering.

Since the mind is the primary factor in meditation, our attitude is also very important. This is why the Buddha taught that we should try to develop an altruistic attitude of thinking more in terms of others than in terms of ourselves. Usually we try to attain personal happiness with a very egotistic attitude. Through such an attitude it is impossible to achieve happiness because this egotistical happiness will involve harming others. In fact, we will never be able to achieve happiness in a selfish way because we will meet too many obstacles. On the contrary, having benevolence for others will result in our own happiness and the happiness of others. This is why the Buddha stressed the great importance of trying to think more of others and less of ourselves. This is embodied by bodhichitta, a mind that is intent on enlightenment for the sake of all other beings.

Cutting Thoughts

We saw in the previous chapter that the first thing to do in meditation is to let the mind remain within its own condition. This is the basic technique for the meditation without a support. Now we come to the actual technique to be used while we are meditating in this way. When we are meditating, surreptitiously thoughts will creep in, but we may not be aware of them. Then all of a sudden, we realize that we have been distracted. This thought could be a thought of the past or the future. This thought creeps in very surreptitiously and develops quickly, so what do we do?

When a thought creeps in, we have to cut through it immediately and completely. This involves maintaining enough mindfulness to see the thought when it comes up. Once a thought creeps into the mind, we shouldn't get involved with the thought or follow it, because if we do, the thought will trigger another thought, and that will trigger yet another one, so that we will end up being completely distracted with our mind running wild. When a thought arises, we must immediately cut it short without any involvement with the thought. We can do this partly by realizing there is no benefit to becoming involved with thought—all we have to do is to continue on with meditation.

We must be sure that we understand what is meant by this term "to cut the thought short." It doesn't mean to repress the thought and keep on fighting it. When a thought comes up, it is a matter of becoming directly aware of the presence of the thought. If we try to stop the thought and to fight it, this isn't meditation because forcibly repressing thoughts will make the mind very tense and uneasy, or in extreme cases even make us feel physically unwell. By cutting thoughts short we are not speaking of repressing thoughts.

When meditators of the past practiced, the meditation didn't make them feel more unhappy or bring them more difficulties; it brought them great peace. We can also achieve this peace. Cutting short the thoughts doesn't mean repressing them, but rather means becoming aware of the presence of the thought when it comes up. We recognize the fact that now we are thinking, so it's a matter of having very sharp awareness and mindfulness. Once we are aware of the presence of the thought, the point is not to become involved with the thoughts. An example of what not to do would be to think of someone who is criticizing us and let this angry thought make us think of what we can say back to the person. Because of this angry feeling, we become involved with the thought of wanting to get back at the person and we keep elaborating on it. If we do this, then it's of no benefit to our meditation and all we are doing is creating a lot of disturbance in our mind.

Rather than trying to stop thoughts or repress them, what we have to do is let go and relax; within this relaxation and letting go, the thought will just vanish automatically. Therefore, we shouldn't misunderstand cutting thoughts short as stopping or repressing thoughts, but as relaxing the mind, so that the thoughts can just vanish.

When we apply the technique of cutting the thought short, we have a quick recognition of the presence of the thought. When the thought arises, it is a factor of disturbance because the mind won't feel very comfortable once the thought is there. However, most of the time we do not recognize the presence of thought. Just think of what has happened to us since we got up this morning. From the moment we got up until now, there has been an uninterrupted river of thoughts, one thought after another. We are not aware of just how many thoughts have been going on; we don't know what thought came first and then which one followed it and so on. Even if we consider the last hour, there has been an uninterrupted flow of thoughts, but we are totally unaware of what has been going on in our mind. We can't recognize these thoughts; we can't identify most of the thoughts.

The reason for the lack of unawareness of our thoughts is that we were carried away and became distracted by them. In the end there are so many thoughts that we didn't even know what they were or how many there were. What we need is a sharper mindfulness and awareness. When a thought appears, we actually know that we are thinking. The purpose of meditation is to know our thoughts and to recognize them when they arise. Besides recognizing them, there must also be noninvolvement in them. Even though we may be aware of the thought coming up, if we follow the thought, we just become distracted. But if we recognize the thought and do not become involved with it, the thought will dissolve.

It is very important to become aware of thoughts as soon as they arise. An example of this often quoted in books on meditation is the example of a pig. If you pull a pig with a chain in its nose into a field to make it eat vegetables in the field, the pig will probably not do so because the chain in the nose is very painful and the pain will take away the pig's interest in tasting anything. But if the pig has escaped into the field by itself and started eating the vegetables, once it has tasted the plants, there would be no way to get the pig out of the garden without a lot of force.

In the same way, if you can be aware of the thought as soon as it arises in the mind, there is no time for involvement to take place, and it is very easy to let go of the thought. But if you let the thought go on for a long time, then you become involved with it and at that point it is very difficult to let go of it. That is why it is absolutely vital to recognize the presence of the thought as soon as it appears in the mind.

Sometimes when we meditate, it seems to us that meditation increases the number of thoughts we have. Actually, there has always been an uninterrupted flow of thoughts in our mind. The difference is that we were unaware of any of this. We couldn't even tell that there was a thought in our mind and that it was triggering another one. However, when we started practicing meditation, we began acknowledging the presence of thought. When we meditate, we can see that now there is a thought, now another one. We have the feeling that we are thinking a lot more, but we are not; it's just that now we are aware that we are thinking. We shouldn't feel that because we are thinking more, our meditation is getting worse. On the contrary, it is getting better. This recognition of having a lot of thoughts is in fact the first sign that our meditation is developing.

Stages of Tranquillity Meditation

There are different stages of meditation in terms of the different levels of tranquillity that can be achieved. There are three basic levels. The first level is compared to a mountain stream which is running down a steep mountain, so that the water is quite agitated with lots of movement in it. All the time we have been in samsara, which has been for a very long time, our mind has been involved with outer things. Because we've been used to so much thinking and relating to outer things, it is very difficult for us to have a quiet and still mind overnight. At the first level of tranquillity we become aware of thoughts. The second level is that of a great meandering river and the final level is compared to a great ocean. These stages will be described in the following chapters.

Normally, when we receive teachings, it's beneficial to think about them over and over again, and even retake these teachings until we have much more understanding of them. But when it comes to meditation, the most important thing is not to hear more about it or think about it, but to experience it with practice.

Questions

Question: When sitting in meditation my body sometimes gets very hot or I get a funny kind of tingling in the end of my fingers. Why does this happen?
Rinpoche: When we meditate we need to be extremely relaxed both physically and mentally. Sometimes when we are not quite relaxed enough, we will get different kinds of feelings, and this feeling of heat could be one of them. If you can relax more in your meditation, there will be no particular strange feeling in your meditation.

Chart 3

The Six Obstacles and the Eight Remedies

The Obstacles*	The Antidotes
1. Laziness (There are three kinds: An interest in only sleeping, too much attachment to worldly things so one has no interest in dharma, and self-deprecation thinking, "I'm not capable of following the path.")	1. Appreciation of Dharma
	2. Diligence and Faith 3. Faith 4. Workability
2. Forgetting the Instructions (Not remembering what one is taught)	5. Mindfulness
3. Drowsiness and Agitation (The mind is either in a state of lethargy or sleepiness or it is over-stimulated by thoughts)	6. Awareness and then applying the proper antidote
4. Under-application (One doesn't apply the remedies when one is drowsy or too stimulated.)	7. Awareness
5. Over-application (One applies the remedies described above even when one doesn't need them.)	8. Rest in Meditative State

* The five obstacles were originally described in Maitreya's *Distinguishing the Middle from the Extremes.*

Chapter 9

Noninterference with Thoughts

Raising Bodhichitta

Please try to listen to this teaching[19] with a mind that is truly intent on perfect enlightenment for the sake of other beings. In other words, try to have a pure motivation. This is very important when we listen to the teachings and it is also important at all other times. We have to try to align our thinking with the Dharma. At all times we must act in a way that it is beneficial for ourselves and for others. If we don't make any effort to practice, then we are not going to find any improvement in our mind. To improve ourselves we need to practice. Of course, we all know this. That is why we come here to listen to the teachings and to learn how to practice. That is why I try to explain to you whatever I know about the Dharma.

We should receive these teachings in such a way that really helps us to reduce our negativity and helps us to increase our qualities of meditation and compassion. This requires a certain amount of effort. When we are actually listening to the teachings, we must make even more effort than usual to focus. This is the time when our faith and devotion must be very strong, when our feeling of compassion and bodhichitta must be very alive, and when we must try not to become involved in any negativity that may come up. Of course, there will be negative thoughts arising in our mind, but we mustn't feel bad about it because we have been living in samsara for so long. This has been such a long-lasting habit that it is hard for negative thoughts not to arise, but we still must make an effort, particularly during teachings.

For instance, if we feel very strong anger, we make an effort not to act it out. If we do this again and again, in the end the anger will diminish. This is what we need to do and this actually is taking responsibility for our own mind. We have to find out what our problems are, what our obstacles are, and try to get rid of them. We also have to try to see what's good in us and develop this more.

We are told that we must try to love other people, but this begins with loving ourselves first, with being kind to ourselves. We mustn't subject ourselves to suffering, we mustn't forget that we have good qualities. This implies that we must try to get rid of unhelpful faults in order to be able to achieve really good results and helpful qualities. That is why when we listen to teachings we must try not to be casual or careless about it, but put a lot of effort into it and practice with very great diligence.

We should realize that when we listen to teachings it is not just a matter of what is said in words. If we hear that we mustn't have anger, we must try to get rid of anger. If we take it to be just words, then we won't really care what is going on in our mind. We hear, "They say you mustn't have anger," but in our mind we don't care whether we are angry or not. If we act in such a way, it doesn't mean that the teaching we received has no benefit at all, but it isn't of very much benefit if the teaching is not put into practice.

We shouldn't feel that Dharma occurs only when we sit down and meditate. Dharma should be present with us all the time. Dharma should be practiced in everything we do and at all times and used in all our actions. Of course, at the moment we can't act like Milarepa and the Buddha, but at least we can try to be responsible for our own mind. We must try our best not to let the negative mental states develop. We must try to feel more compassion, to develop more bodhichitta. Although we can't do this immediately, at least we can do whatever we can by doing it everyday, again and again.

So we shouldn't feel that there is one moment for receiving teachings and another moment for practice, and that these two situations are totally different. Whatever we learn, we have to try to put into practice. However, we shouldn't feel that this is something terribly difficult. When we are told that we should try to get rid of desire, anger, and jealousy, it isn't as though we are being told to give up something nice and pleasant. These mental states are only a source of pain and suffering and therefore are things that we must try to eliminate. On the other hand, when we are taught to try to develop more compassion and all the other beneficial qualities, the true source of goodness and happiness, it is because this leads to true happiness. So in a way it isn't that difficult to develop good qualities, because we can gain from these positive qualities. It isn't that difficult to give up negative qualities, because we know they are harmful and lead to eventual unhappiness. We should really make an effort to put this into practice, not let it just be words but an actuality.

Noninterference with Thoughts in Meditation

In the previous chapter we found that the first instruction of meditation of the Middle-way is to immediately cut short whatever thought arises. By doing this, we can find out what is the borderline between the presence of a thought and the absence of a thought, between what is true meditation and what is not meditation. This makes it possible to eliminate the faults in meditation and to improve whatever is good in the meditation. This is the first step in learning how to meditate without support.

The second method is not to interfere with whatever appears. At first it may sound as if there's a great contradiction between the first and the second technique. Cutting a thought appears to be the opposite to leaving it alone. However, there is no contradiction between these two techniques in what they actually achieve for the mind. In the first technique, we are taught to look straight at the thought, to recognize it. Once we've acknowledged its presence, we just let go of it and then remain very relaxed within this. The second technique of not interfering doesn't mean that if we have a thought of anger or desire or jealousy, we don't do anything letting it grow larger and larger. Rather we simply don't own the thought by thinking, "This is my thought." We don't make any effort to change the situation, but just let go completely without interfering, without modifying anything, so the thought will just dissolves on its own accord.

In this connection, the great mahasiddha Saraha said that if you try to tie up the mind, forcing it to remain in one place, the mind will try to go everywhere. But if you don't tie up the mind or repress it in any way, then it won't go anywhere. The mind won't feel like doing anything because there is nowhere for it to go. It will just remain very naturally as it is. This is traditionally compared to the way in which you should deal with camels. It is very difficult to tie up camels because they are very strong animals and they don't like being tied up. But if you just leave the camel alone it will not wander very far away. It will just remain there. In the same way, you must just relax within the mind, and then it will just stay as it is without any problem.

Shawadipa, Saraha's disciple, asked Saraha to explain how he could actually meditate without interfering with his mind. Saraha explained to him that the mind is by nature unmodified, and being unmodified, it is fresh. There are two ways of modifying the mind. The first way is to think, "I must meditate, I must give up thought" and this very thought modifies the mind. The second way occurs when the mind is always disturbed by all sorts of feelings and thoughts, and this creates a disturbance of the actual nature of the mind, its original state. It is constantly modified and altered by these thoughts and feelings. These are two ways in which the mind is modified or contrived. What Saraha said to Shawadipa is that we must remain within the unmodified nature of the mind. So whatever is there in mind, just be within it. There's no need to change anything.

Another aspect of mind is that it is fresh, it is new. For example, if we've worn clothes for a long time and we've washed them many times, this has modified the clothes. So instead of having the clothes in their original freshness and newness, they have become old. In the same way, the mind has been changed or modified from its original state by following thoughts and being engaged in negative mental states. We have changed our mind a lot, and the result of this is that it is an old mind, no longer fresh, new, and crisp. When Saraha told Shawadipa that he should rest within the freshness, the newness of mind, he meant that we must remain within mind as it is, the nowness of this particular instant of mind. We should be in the moment without corruption by any thought, without any modification. This then is the way not to interfere with whatever arises. If we can remain in the freshness of mind, realization will arise. This realization is not just one instant of realization, but as we become more and more familiar with mind, it becomes real realization.

In this real realization there is no more idea of "I must do this, I must try to find happiness, I must find clarity, I must find emptiness, or I must not do that." There is no longer any idea of anything to achieve or not achieve. It's just a matter of remaining in exactly what is there without changing anything. Saraha concluded this is how the yogi must meditate: not to interfere with whatever happens, not to change anything, and just remain very relaxed within this state.

Gampopa on the same subject said that when we don't change anything in the mind, the mind feels very good and happy. It is very much like clear water. When we do not stir water with dirt on the bottom, the water remains very clear. But if we start stirring it, the water becomes muddy and unclear. Similarly if the mind is left in relaxation, then it is very clear and happy.

How do we meditate without interference? The answer is to just let go. It is not to tie ourselves up in a strait-jacket, and try to interfere and change things, to think in terms of "I must do this" or "I mustn't do that." If we can let go, thoughts will pacify themselves automatically and then the essence of mind is seen very clearly, in all its clarity. In the same way, if the water is not stirred, we can see very clearly, because the water is extremely clear and transparent. Similarly, when the mind is not disturbed by any kind of interference, thoughts just vanish of their own accord, and the mind is left very clear.

Practically speaking, how do we do this meditation? When we are meditating and a thought comes up, the first thing to do is to recognize the thought. Once we have recognized the thought, don't think, "Oh, this is a thought. It's bad. I must stop it. I'm not allowed to follow it." Rather once we've recognized the thought, we just relax within the thought. If we do this, we will find that it just vanishes very naturally itself. Once we can do this, there will be a very natural tranquillity of mind, a great concentration. Even if we wanted to make another thought come at this point, it just wouldn't come, because the mind has come to a very natural state of concentration. However, when another thought does arise, it won't be quite as strong or quite as solid as before. If we practice in this way, we will achieve what is known as the second level of stability. The first step of stability is compared to a mountain stream that is cascading down a mountain quite wildly. This second level of stability is compared to the leisurely flow of a great river. When a great river is flowing, it is not completely still, but is moving all the time steadily and smoothly without any strong disturbances or waves. At the second stage there are still thoughts, but they are not as powerful as before, and they do not create the same strong disturbances as they did before. So this is the second or middle level of tranquillity.

Chapter 10

The Right Tension with Thoughts

The first meditation instruction is to cut short anything that arises suddenly. The second instruction is not to interfere with whatever occurs. The reason we need the first technique is that for a very long time we've been in conditioned existence and we have formed bad habits. That is why when we first begin to meditate, we have to put effort into it trying to concentrate the mind because if we let the mind be too relaxed, we then just fall back into a confused state, losing the thread of meditation. That is why we must cut short whatever arises.

But then there is always the risk that our concentration will make the mind too tight, which is another way of losing the thread of meditation. We have to learn how to relax more, which is the purpose of the second technique of not tightening up. This technique is intended to teach us how we can just let go without interfering with whatever happens. These two techniques are to correct the defect of being too relaxed or being too tight in our meditation.

In using these two methods we might use the first method too much, causing tightness in our meditation, or use the second method too much and not make enough effort in meditation. Then we might encounter struggles in our meditation because we do not know quite how to find the right balance between concentration and relaxation. At this point the third instruction will help us find the right balance between relaxation and concentration. This third technique has four different aspects to it that are illustrated by examples.

The Right Tension in Meditation

When we meditate, we have to try to strike the right balance between keeping our mind too tight or too loose. What is wrong with being too tight in meditation? If we examine our meditation too much, if we take too much care to the point that we are always interfering with the meditation by wondering whether we are actually doing it right. We won't allow the mind to rest and the meditation will be lost through too much investigating. But we may make the opposite mistake of being too relaxed in our meditation. Are we really in control of our meditation? Are we identifying any problems in our meditation so that we can correct them? Without looking at our meditation, our thoughts will become very wild or very dull, and in the end it will be as if we had never meditated. If we don't examine our meditation enough for its qualities and defects, our thoughts will become coarse and keep us from progressing. Our meditation will become more and more confused. That is why it is very important to find the right balance between being too tight and too loose in meditation.

To keep a balance between the tension and relaxation in meditation, we should keep them equal all the time. The great mahasiddha, Saraha, explained how to keep this balance with the example of a Brahmin spinning thread. The Brahmins of his day wore a red cord which they spun themselves. When spinning thread, if one spins it too tight, it won't be very good because it will snap easily. However, if one spins without enough tension in the thread, the thread won't hold together properly and will unravel. By making a thread with exactly the right amount of tension, we will have the best quality thread that is very soft, smooth, workable, and resilient. In the same way, when we meditate, there shouldn't be too much tightness or too much looseness because tension will create agitation and give rise to many thoughts, while looseness will cause us to become drowsy and dull.

When we say to be more relaxed in meditation we do not mean that when a thought arises, we should let it develop and follow it. No, we don't let the thoughts go wild and develop and lead us astray. Relaxing the mind means returning to the true nature of the mind. The sutras speak of mind as being the very essence of emptiness, not having any real solid existence, but being clear and empty at the same time. The tantras of the vajrayana speak of the true nature of the mind as being beyond anything the intellect can conceive. Whatever terms are used to describe mind they are always speaking of the same thing, which is the natural state or true nature of mind. In fact, if the Buddha hadn't said the mind was empty, it wouldn't have made any difference because emptiness is part of the nature of the mind. Whether we meditate on the true nature of mind or not, it's not going to modify the nature of the mind itself. The mind is not modified by thoughts, but is clear and conscious. When we say that the mind is empty, it isn't the kind of emptiness that is completely void.[20]

When looking at the mind, it's not a matter of just following thoughts thinking, "That's one thought," and the next instant thinking, "Here comes the second thought," and so on. Rather it's a matter of looking directly[21] at what is happening within the instant when we're looking. Here we are not employing an analytical approach using logic, but we are looking directly into the essence of the mind. If we can just directly look at what is there, then the thoughts automatically vanish of their own accord. This is what is meant by letting go in meditation.

Relaxing the mind when negative factors disturb our mind is done by not repressing these thoughts forcibly, but letting them go. For example, we may be thinking of someone who upsets us and the feeling of anger is extremely vivid, very solid, and completely unbearable. We feel that we must do something; we must either scream or fight because we can't take it. But, in fact, what is this anger? If we look at it closely, we will see that it is not part of the nature of the mind; it is just there while the mind is engaged in relating to outer things. When the mind is distracted and not aware of what is going on in itself, then these feelings appear like bubbles on the surface of the water. When we examine the anger, we shouldn't try to do so in abstract terms as if thinking of yesterday's anger. We examine it at the moment that we are angry. We try to look straight into the essence of that anger and ask, "Where does it come from? Where does it go? What is it? Does it have any form, any shape, and any color? Is it outside or inside of us? Where does this unbearable feeling come from?"

If we are able to look at the anger very directly, then automatically it will disappear. Even though the feeling of anger vanishes, the clarity (or intelligence) of the mind remains, because clarity is the very essence of mind. Anger can vanish because it doesn't have any substantial nature. In the face of thoughts or negative feelings, we shouldn't try to give them up or to fight them. All we have to do is look at them directly and they will just vanish.

The example of looking directly at anger is also true for other problems, such as desire or attachment. We may have all sorts of attachment, such as being involved with our person, our possessions, our money, our friends, or our family. This feeling of attachment is very strong, very solid, and continually present. We feel that we can't let go of it because the attachment is really very strong. As the days go by, this feeling gets stronger and more vivid. But, in fact, what we have to do is to look directly into its essence, try to see directly what it is. This can be done through examining the nature of mind. Then we will see nothing that we can pinpoint as being this or that. There is nothing we can find, and at that moment, it just dissolves.

The technique of direct looking is also the way to deal with feelings. We may have physical or mental sensations that produce either pleasant or unpleasant feelings. We may feel, "Oh, today has been going very nicely," and we will have a very happy feeling. However, if we consider this happy feeling, it is only an idea. If we look into the mind, we won't find this "I like" or "I'm happy" feeling anywhere in the mind. It is obvious that this feeling is empty of inherent existence,[22] in that there is no such thing in our mind. The same thing is true of physical and mental pain. If, for example, we have mental pain which is really unbearable, we look at it right at that moment and ask, "Where is the pain?" and "How have I got pain in my mind?" there will be nothing there; it will vanish. In both cases we just let go, ease ourselves into the nature of mind. In that way we will avoid becoming involved with whatever feelings we have. If we have pleasant feelings, we won't become attached to them; or if we have painful feelings, we won't be frightened by them.

If we can ease into the nature of mind, then all our pleasant and unpleasant feelings will simply vanish and all disturbing factors that distress our mind will also disappear. This is because the bondage of thoughts and feelings in our mind is not real, but only fabricated by our ideas. Once we know this, negative feelings go away on their own accord. That is why, when we meditate and try to face our negativity, we shouldn't try to be tense or forceful or try to stop our thoughts or feelings, but should just let go within the nature of mind.

These thoughts in our mind include thoughts of pain as well. When we are not very experienced at meditation, it is quite difficult to look at the essence of physical pain and understand that it's not there. But we can begin with very little pain, like what we experience when we pinch our skin. At first there will be the feeling of pain because this is a consequence of interdependent origination.[23] If we believe the pinching is going to be felt inside, there will be some pain. But if we can look right into the essence of that pain, we will find that it is not as unbearable as it seems to be. While we are looking at it directly, we will find that the feeling of pain actually diminishes, until at the end it is not there at all. If we can do this with small pain, we can become more and more familiar with this technique, until we can use it with greater pain.

The Nature of the Illusion

When we began many lifetimes ago, we made the mistake of taking thoughts to be the true nature of mind. Then we made the mistake of becoming more and more deeply involved in this illusion until we took the illusion to be our present reality. The technical explanation given in the Abhidharma is that the first form of illusion began with the *ground consciousness* (Skt. *alaya*).[24] At the beginning the alaya consciousness had only a slight form of an illusion because it was still lucid and cognizant. But then it became thicker and began to form an intellect. From the intellect, the illusion develops further so that outer objects and the senses were perceived as external objects. It is more difficult to put up with physical pain than with psychological pain, because the level of illusion on which we find tactile perception is much coarser than intellectual perception. Physical pain is like the highest degree of illusion, the densest.

The Right Timing with Thoughts

We continue with the third method of dealing with thoughts in tranquillity meditation. The first method is to cut short whatever arises suddenly in the mind. The second method is not to interfere with anything that may go on in the mind. This third method is dealing with subtle thoughts and we use a set of four techniques. The first technique given in the previous section is to find the right tension between the mind being too tense or too loose. This was illustrated by the example of a Brahmin spinning thread.

We must employ this system of instructions not only when we meditate, but also at other times when our mind is constantly busy with thoughts. This is because since beginningless time we have been in samsara, our mind has been used to going in all directions. Once we stabilize our thoughts a little, we become aware of the thoughts arising. This second technique is exercising mindfulness after a thought has arisen.

Dealing with a Thought that has Arisen

We learned through the two previous methods how cutting a thought short and not interfering with it to apply the right kind of remedy to thoughts arising in meditation. There is always the possibility that once thoughts arise in meditation, we become aware of the thought too late and it has already taken shape. We need to know how to apply mindfulness after the thought has already arisen. For example, we may think, "Well, I've just had a thought of desire and then I had a thought of anger and after that I had a very positive thought." So, of course, we know what's been happening during the last few thoughts, but it doesn't improve our meditation. In fact, knowing all this cognizing is going to disturb whatever tranquillity we might have been able to achieve. When we are meditating and a thought comes up, immediately we must let the thought go completely, naturally, of its own accord without thinking, "Now I must let go of the thought."

An example of this second technique is of a string that is tying a bale of straw that snaps. When the string snaps, the original bundle of straw falls apart in a very natural pattern. There would be no point in thinking it has to fall this way or that way, or it has to be a little bit tighter on that side or looser on this side. It will just fall very naturally without any effort involved. In the same way, when thoughts come, one must be aware of the thoughts, but then there is no need for any more effort; just be aware of the thought and then just leave it within the actual nature of mind.

We have to try to let go within the nature of mind without any effort. Why is it important that there is no effort? It is because the actual essence of mind, the natural condition of the mind has not been created in any way. Whether we meditate on it or not, whether the Buddha taught about it or not, whether we understand it or not, it is not going to make any difference to the actual nature of the mind itself. Even if a hundred people say there is a mind that is not going to make the mind any different. It is very much the same as if a hundred people said, "Fire is a very cold thing." Nobody can change it by saying or doing anything. Whatever is there naturally cannot be altered.

How is it then that there are problems in connection with our mind? The mind is naturally very peaceful, very relaxed, clear and lucid, but the problem is that we don't recognize this original nature of mind. We are always turning outward and becoming very involved with thoughts. The mind is then more and more covered up by all sorts of thoughts and ideas. The mind that was originally peaceful, calm, happy, and clear is not evident anymore, because it has been covered up by thoughts and ideas that we indulge in continually.

It's very much like an insect that makes a cocoon. The insect produces a very fine thread around its body and in the end the insect is completely wrapped up in this little cocoon. All our thoughts and ideas create this sort of cocoon or cover around the mind, so that we can't see its pure, clear, and peaceful nature anymore. The only thing to do is to relax completely within the nature of the mind. The thoughts, ideas, confusion, illusion will just go once we're back to the nature of mind.

The point of this second technique of meditation, illustrated by the example of the rope tying the bale of straw, is to show us that when thoughts arise, we must not follow them, but let them go without any kind of effort. When we say "without any kind of effort," it doesn't mean that we do nothing or that we don't care what happens in the meditation. Rather it means to let go within the mind itself.

Dealing with Temporary Experiences

When we say "meditation," we actually mean "cultivation."[25] That is, to practice something in order to become familiar with it. If we practice in this way, the result of practice is experience. Once we practice meditation, there will be three main kinds of temporary experiences (Tib. *nyam*): experiences of bliss, of clarity, and of non-thought. Experiences of happiness mean that from time to time you may feel that your mind is extremely happy, contented, in a very great state of bliss. You may also feel intense bliss in your body. Sometimes it might be very slight, but it's basically the same experience of happiness or bliss. The second experience of clarity is when you have the feeling that your meditation is really very good and clear. Actually what you are experiencing is not the natural state of the mind, but the experience of clarity which results from the power of the meditation. The third experience of non-thought is the moment when you feel there is no thought in your meditation. You may even feel that perhaps your whole body or mind has gone and there is nothing there. It is as if everything has dissolved completely.

What are we to do in the face of these three different kinds of experiences? When we feel great clarity or bliss or non-thought, we feel very happy and we might become attached to the experience. Of course, we must not become attached to these feelings. Similarly, if we have difficult experiences, we might feel that our meditation is really bad, that we aren't getting anywhere, and become discouraged. However, we shouldn't think in terms of good and bad experiences. They are just experiences, and as such, we just have to let go of them in a very relaxed and very natural way.

When we have experiences like the ones just described, we must try not to become involved with the experiences, neither clinging to them nor trying to get rid of them. We don't think it's good or it's bad, but just let them go very naturally. When we meditate we still experience physical perceptions: our eyes can still see, we can still smell, hear, touch, and taste. For instance, sight doesn't stop once we meditate, but when we meditate we should relate to our perceptions in a different way. Normally when we perceive something, we label it as being nice or ugly, as something we like or don't. In meditation, we see things very clearly, but we let them be as they are without labeling them.

In the same way, when we meditate, we can hear nice sounds, unpleasant ones, loud ones, but within the essence of mind there is no difference in terms of a good or a bad sound. We register all sounds, but we don't think in terms of good or bad ones; we just let go. This is true of all our sensory experiences, because the nature of the mind is very clear, very alive, very vivid, and this clarity of mind never stops. That is why all these sensations are possible.

An example of how to deal with these temporary experiences is the way a little baby sees a place, such as a shrine room. A baby cannot talk or think intellectually, so the baby just registers what is there without making judgments or comments on what it experiences. A baby reacts very much like a camera, it just registers whatever is there very clearly taking a picture with no value judgment involved. We're given the advice that when we meditate, whether we experience inner feelings or sensory perceptions, we shouldn't try to stop this experience, but we just let whatever happens go in a very relaxed and very natural way. This is the third example.

Tilopa gave instructions to his disciple, Naropa, by saying, "My son, whatever appears in meditation creates no problems, no trouble, no discomfort. It doesn't obscure the original intelligence of mind. It is just like a rainbow in the sky." It is there, but it makes no difference. What makes a difference? The difference sets in once there is involvement in the form of thoughts, by thinking, "this is nice," or "this is bad," or "this is pleasant," or "I want," or "I don't want." Once the thoughts begin, the mind cannot remain tranquil or relaxed. All these thoughts are obstacles to the mind resting within its own nature. The thoughts alter the natural condition of mind, they obscure it. So Tilopa concluded, "Naropa, you must let go of involvement."

What we learn from this teaching by Tilopa is that when we meditate there is no need to stop whatever is going on outside or inside. There is no need to stop form, sound, smell, taste, touch, and there is no need to stop the inner experiences that we may have. These experiences are due to the clear nature of the mind, but they can just be there vividly, without any need to have any involvement with them or to put any mental label on them. All we need to do is to let go within the essence of these experiences and the involvement will naturally decrease by itself.

Not Being Involved with Thoughts

There are three major instructions used in Middle-way meditation and the third instruction has four techniques, each of which is illustrated by an example. The first technique is finding the right balance between being too loose or too tight in meditation, previously illustrated by the example of the Brahmin spinning his thread. The second technique is exercising mindfulness at just the proper time being not too late, but facing the thought effortlessly and immediately with the right remedy. This is compared to tying a bale of straw with a string that snaps. The third technique is not becoming involved with the sensory perceptions such as form, sound, taste, that you experience in meditation or with experiences of clarity, of happiness, or non-thought. All of these do occur very clearly and vividly to us, but we mustn't become involved with them. This is illustrated by the example of a baby looking at a shrine room.

The fourth technique relates to having an expansive feeling during meditation in which all outer events such as sight and sounds and inner events such as thoughts and feelings simply do not disturb us. Our meditation is so steady and stable that appearances simply don't affect our meditation. The example of this is trying to prick an elephant with a thorn. The elephant has such a thick skin that a thorn will hardly even be noticed by the elephant. Even though there are slight differences in these four techniques, these techniques are all a matter of easing oneself into the essence of mind.

In Tibet the hinayana, mahayana, and vajrayana were taught and all flourished there. The teachings of the first two turnings of the wheel of Dharma, the hinayana and the mahayana teachings, were transmitted to Tibet early in the eighth century. Later on in the twelfth century, the Kagyu lineage beginning with Tilopa, Naropa, Marpa, Milarepa, and Gampopa transmitted a line of oral teachings which were part of the vajrayana. These oral teachings were outlined by Gampopa in *The Jewel Ornament of Liberation*, in which he covered the whole path from the moment one first meets one's spiritual friend and tries to cultivate bodhichitta up to the point where one achieves final realization.

When it comes to practicing the Buddha's teachings, one can practice according to the way of the sutras or the way of the tantras. The sutra approach was outlined in Kamalashila's system of Middle-way meditation, which gives priority to the analytical form of meditation. Here one begins with studying analytical arguments concerning the empty nature of all phenomena. One then tries to rest within this view in meditation to develop certainty about the nature of phenomena.

The vajrayana path in contrast involves the development of tranquillity and insight in meditation. The development of tranquillity meditation was explained in this text when discussing primarily the meditation of letting go. This can be done either with a support or without a support. In the last few chapters we have discussed tranquillity of mind being developed without a support.

The Stages of Meditation

All the stages of meditation are meant to help us increase the stability of our mind and to develop the experience of tranquillity. Stability means to establish it in a very peaceful, smooth state. That's why it is called tranquillity meditation.

In the first method of cutting short the thoughts that arise, one still doesn't have very much experience in meditation and the mind isn't very stable. At this stage there are many thoughts and they are very strong and very coarse. Correspondingly, the remedy that has to be used has to be strong as well, because without a strong remedy there wouldn't be any way to develop any stability of mind and the thread of the meditation would constantly be lost. This stage is compared to a cascade of water running down the side of the mountain moving very fast and chaotically.

The second method of not interfering with whatever goes on in the mind is compared to the leisurely flow of a great river. At this point thoughts still arise, but because one's habit of dealing with them has developed, one no longer tries to use a remedy other than just letting go. Here one relaxes into the essence of mind, its unmodified state. This is possible only because at this point one has established enough tranquillity of mind that there is no longer the need to have a very active remedy; the thoughts are not as coarse and strong as they used to be. At this point the mind is already a lot smoother and more relaxed and peaceful. However, it is not completely without movement because there are still thoughts, but they are not as rough as they used to be. At this stage, the tranquillity is compared to that of the leisurely flow of a great river.

Finally, by developing more and more familiarity with the previous stages, one reaches the last level of tranquillity. This corresponds to the third meditation explained by the four examples. At this point there are no longer any of the problems of excessive tension or excessive looseness in the meditation. There are no longer any problems with obvious, coarse thoughts because these now have gone. This last stage of meditation is concerned with very fine, subtle thoughts. At this point, one's mind has become so fine that one can't actually tell whether one is thinking or not. These last four techniques are meant to help one find if there are any very fine thoughts there or not. At this point we are dealing with thoughts so fine, so subtle that one can't use any of the gross techniques of previous stages. Instead, it is a matter of being aware of the presence or absence of these very, very slight movements of mind. This is achieved primarily through relaxing into the mind's essence. In the first example of the Brahmin spinning his thread, one establishes the right balance between tension and looseness. The second, third, and fourth steps are mainly just a matter of relaxing within the essence of mind. This is the way to achieve the pacification of all forms of thoughts, especially the very subtle ones. The level of tranquillity that is achieved at this fourth step of the third method is compared to the example of the stillness of the ocean without any waves. In the previous stage, the tranquillity was compared to a great river that wasn't agitated, but because it was flowing, there were constant ripples on the surface. Now the ocean is not flowing because it remains where it is and is not disturbed by any wind making waves on its surface. By letting go completely within the mind, one achieves this very great stability.

As we become more and more familiar with tranquillity, it will develop further and further and become very stable. This stability of mind helps us see the essence of mind very clearly.

Questions

Question: Could you explain more about the mind being lucid and cognizant?

Rinpoche: When we say that the nature of mind is both lucid and cognizant, we mean practically the same thing. In general, we find the mind to be empty, lucid, and conscious. When we examine it with a discerning intelligence (Skt. *prajna*), not in terms of meditative experience, we find that the mind is empty. We mean that when we look for the mind, we can't find it, so this not finding the mind is the emptiness of mind. Then when we say the mind has lucidity or luminosity (Tib. *salwa*) we mean the mind can know, it can feel, it can experience. It's not like a stone or dead object, so this lucid aspect of the mind is, in fact, very close to the next aspect, being conscious or cognizant, which means it can know things, it can feel them, it can understand.

Question: How do we meditate on emptiness in the vajrayana?

Rinpoche: Actually the goal of all meditation is to realize the true nature of all phenomena, but in vajrayana one uses a special technique, which is to meditate on the true nature of the mind. This is because it would be extremely difficult for us to meditate on the nature of phenomena to begin with. We do not have any kind of habit of relating to phenomena in this way and it would be extremely difficult to understand this directly. The vajrayana meditates on the true nature of the mind, because the nature of mind and the nature of phenomena are not two different things. They are one and the same, so that if we can realize the true nature of the mind, we automatically have realized the true nature of all phenomena. But when we say the true nature of mind, we shouldn't think of the mind and its nature as being two separate things, such as the mind being one thing, which is white and its nature being another thing that is black. It's not two things. We're just speaking of what the mind really is in its natural state, its natural condition. While we are ignorant about this true condition of the mind, we fall under the influence of all the various negative factors that create a lot of distress and disturbance in the mind. Once we know what the mind actually is, then we will automatically see what all things are.[26]

Chapter 11

Insight Meditation in the Middle-way

Once we have established the mind in tranquillity, we look at the essence of mind and see that the mind is clear, lucid, not agitated by thoughts, and very relaxed. Then a thought comes. Before we've engaged the thought, usually making a value judgment about it, we find it difficult to just recognize it as a thought. Then what we have to do is to see exactly what is happening once a thought arises. How does that affect the essence or the original state of mind? When a thought arises, how does that modify the essence of mind? Then when there is no thought and the mind is at rest, how does that modify its essence? This is what we have to investigate. So when a thought arises, is there any change in the nature of the mind? Also when there is no thought, is there any difference in the nature of the mind?

Actually we will find with careful and repeated examination that we cannot detect any difference between the moment when there is a thought in the mind and when there is no thought, insofar as the essence of the mind is concerned. But this is what we have to investigate. When a thought arises, we try to see how the arising of the thought modifies or doesn't modify the essence of mind. When the mind is at rest, we see how the calm abiding of our tranquillity meditation modifies or doesn't modify the essence of mind. If we find there is no difference, then we must try to realize how there is no difference within the essence of mind. This is the way to understand the tranquil and lucid essence of mind.

Before we begin to meditate, it would seem to us that there is a great deal of difference between the moment when the mind is tranquil and the moment when it is agitated by thoughts. It is true, we experience these two as very different states of mind. There is a great deal of difference in these conditions because we have had so many thoughts that we haven't managed to gain much realization.

But once stability has been gained with real meditation, there is no longer any difference between a mind at rest and a mind in movement. This is because within the essence of mind, movement and tranquillity are both included. Whether a thought has arisen or the mind is at rest makes absolutely no difference to the essence of mind. Once we recognize this, having thoughts is part of meditation because we are still resting within the essence of mind. As we become better meditators, the gap between resting and agitation is reduced so much that in the end it vanishes completely. Whether our mind is very peaceful or agitated by thoughts, we still are in the same state of meditation. Once we understand this we wonder why we couldn't understand what meditation was before. We probably feel that meditation was something very far off and difficult. In fact, it is simply like going back home, going back to the essence of mind.

Devotion

In the development of meditation, devotion for the Buddha, the bodhisattvas, Dharma, and one's lineage and one's root guru is very important. There are two reasons why devotion is important. First, devotion comes from a very strong feeling of faith and aspiration. This in turn gives rise to great diligence, and makes one work hard at the goal without obstacles. However, if one has no devotion, there won't be any diligence and there won't be much result.

Second, if someone who has a general sense of devotion receives meditation instruction and tries to practice, he or she will feel great devotion towards the meditation itself and great trust in meditation. With this feeling it is possible to really develop one's experience of meditation because one feels that meditation is alive, that it's becoming clearer, that it's becoming stronger. This will help one to experience the feeling of blessing. This is important because once one has the feeling of devotion in meditation, this feeling of blessings will automatically have the power to clarify one's meditation. It can dispel thoughts, it can remove problems in meditation through a clear feeling of devotion and blessing, so the meditation becomes very clear, very quickly. That is why faith and devotion are important for the practice in general and essential for the meditation practice. It is said that devotion is actually the key to the mind. With faith and devotion, one can open the door that leads to knowing the true nature of the mind. That is why one should make sure that there is this feeling of faith and devotion and feeling of blessing in the meditation.

Compassion

The practice of meditation will make one a better person. It is said that emptiness is the essence of compassion, so if we have some realization of the true nature of mind, we will automatically feel compassion for other beings who have not had the chance to develop meditation and haven't realized the nature of mind. This all comes through the power of meditation. The more we understand through meditation, the more we will have compassion and be benevolent towards others. The more the mind feels comfortable and relaxed, the less it will be disturbed by any form of negativity.

However, when some people practice, they seem to go from bad to worse and meet with lots of difficulties, with their negativity becoming greater and greater: They become more and more angry, more and more proud, or more and more stupid. This isn't a sign of true meditation. They feel less and less in harmony with other people who are practicing. They feel that they want to be on their own and not mix with other people. All these are signs of improper practice because when meditation truly develops, the mind becomes more and more peaceful, more and more well controlled. One becomes more and more benevolent and loving towards other beings. This is the direct result of true meditation. When we practice meditation, we should try to do it in the spirit that leads to true qualities of meditation and not to the kind of meditation where one forgets about proper and wholesome things. When we practice meditation, we should try to do it in the right way, so that the mind becomes more peaceful and more relaxed. If we can learn to tame our mind, then automatically all our actions will become better, too. With a tamed mind, we become a better person for others to be with and have a much happier and more peaceful mind ourselves.

The Middle-way Meditation Instructions

Chapter 12

The Middle-way Practice in the Vajrayana

Hinduism believes in gods that manifest sometimes peacefully and sometimes wrathfully. It is believed that if one makes offerings and prays to them, they will bestow various spiritual accomplishments that are required to obtain liberation. Theistic religions such as Hinduism are not a wrong path, but they are a path that gradually, through faith and devotion, leads one to the true path of real understanding. In the Theravada school of Buddhism, the emphasis is completely the opposite. According to Theravada practice, there are no gods or deities of any kind. The only thing that matters is to meditate on the natural state of the mind. This again is not a wrong path either, but a path which, through developing tranquillity and insight in the mind, leads one to benefiting others and to the achievement of liberation. This is also a path that leads to goodness and therefore doesn't lead to anything wrong or harmful.

The most prominent school of Buddhism practiced in Tibet was the vajrayana. But actually the Buddhism of Tibet is known as the "threefold vajra," meaning the practice that accomplishes the three vehicles. All three vehicles were practiced within one method of practice. In the vajrayana, a deity is not understood as something external, outside of oneself, but something that is part of one's mind, something that can be realized within the mind. We all have Buddha-nature or Buddha-essence, and this Buddha-nature is the very expression of all the positive qualities of the Buddha, such as loving-kindness, compassion, bodhichitta, the wisdom of the true nature of phenomena, and the wisdom of the variety of phenomena. In our present state as an unenlightened person, our positive qualities are hidden, covered up by impurities. But when the impurities are removed, the positive qualities manifest. Whether we actually use techniques of deity practice or not makes no difference in achieving enlightenment, because all we are doing in all spiritual practices is just uncovering what is already there.

Yidam Practice

In Tibetan Buddhism there are deity or *yidam* practices which involve the visualization of different yidams. Some yidam practices have to do with peaceful yidams and others concern very forceful yidams called wrathful yidams. Some of the peaceful yidams appear full of desire and attachment and are depicted in sexual union and some of the wrathful yidams are depicted as being very angry and frightening. We can see the different representations of these deities[26] in the *thangkas*. In the vajrayana, there are practices related to lamas, practices related to yidams, and also meditation instructions on meditating on the essence of mind with no need for yidams. This latter practice may appear to be a contradiction to the yidam practice. In the vajrayana we describe the *creation stage* (Tib. *che rim*), or the stage of visualization, as the practice in which one imagines a deity and prays to that deity as a way to receive his or her blessings. This blessing is the way to achieve experience and realization. But we may well also be taught that there is no need to pray to any deities, that seeking external help leads to no benefit, and that what matters is to meditate directly on the essence of mind. Seeing a contradiction in this can cause great doubts. We will explain this seeming contradiction in relation to the particular aspect which is the mandala of the yidams.

The Three Aspects of Yidam Deities

There are many different kinds of deities or yidams, such as Chenrezig (Skt. *Avalokiteshvara*), Tara, Dorje Palmo (Skt. *Vajrayogini*) and so forth. But we can describe all of these different yidams in relation to three different aspects: the real yidam, the sign yidam, and the symbolic yidam.

For instance, applying this first aspect, the real yidam, to Chenrezig means that Chenrezig is not something external to us. Chenresig is the very expression of compassion within our mind.

When this compassion has been fully developed, it becomes universal compassion, which is without any conceptual reference, spontaneously present for all beings. When we have this kind of realization, Chenrezig's form becomes truly manifest. It's definitely not something outside of oneself, but within oneself. It is the very expression of great compassion.

The yidam can also be a sign of the ultimate accomplishment that one can reach. For example, Chenrezig is the sign of the ultimate accomplishment of compassion. There are Buddhas and bodhisattvas that have achieved the sign aspect of the yidams. They are the indication of what we can achieve if we can practice properly and also a sign of the fact that we also possess these qualities within us. For example, Chenrezig is the quality of compassion that is inherent to our Buddha-nature. The Buddhas and bodhisattvas represent this sign deity, which shows us that we can also bring forth these qualities in us.

Through the power of the wishes of the Buddhas and bodhisattvas and through the power of our own devotion and faith, we can receive their blessings. However, the Buddhas can't just take us out of samsara, like taking a stone out of the fire. This liberation happens only through the meeting of our devotion with their desire to help all beings. This conjunction makes it possible for us to enter the right path. Once we are on the path, we will be able to develop realization and finally achieve all the qualities of purity and complete realization. This is why for the yidam to completely manifest inside us, we pray to the sign aspect of the yidam. Through the yidam's blessing we can come more quickly to the point where the real yidam within us manifests.

The third aspect of the yidam is the symbolic yidam. We have the real yidam within us, but we cannot realize this just now and are not able to experience this directly, so we need some way of making a link or connection with it. In the same way, the sign yidams, that is the Buddhas and bodhisattvas, appear still separate from us. We do not have any direct connection with them. So we need to make a link both with the sign yidam of the Buddhas and bodhisattvas and the real yidam within ourselves. The way we do this is through symbols. Imagine that we are about a hundred feet away from somebody out of talking range. So what we do is use a symbol, a gesture, like waving our hand to say, "Come here." Then the other person understands our signal and walks up to us. Once we are together, the connection is established, and we can talk. In the same way these symbols provide the link we need with the Buddhas and bodhisattvas, between the sign yidam and with the true nature of our mind, the real yidam. For instance, Chenrezig being white, with one face, four hands, and in the vajra posture doesn't mean that Chenrezig is forever frozen in this seated position and always has four hands. All these symbols have a special significance expressing Chenrezig's purity. When we meditate on this symbolic yidam, gradually we will come into contact with, and relate to Chenrezig as representing the Buddhas and bodhisattvas, and to the inner Chenrezig in our mind.

At first it may seem that these three aspects of the yidam are separate, but as we practice, we can see that actually they are all interconnected, with the final result being the fruition of all three coming together. Through meditating on the symbolic yidam, we can come into contact with the sign yidam and receive that blessing, and through receiving that blessing we are able to make the real yidam within our mind manifest. It is through the interconnection of the three that we can truly achieve the goal and this is the reason why we practice visualization.

Visualization of a deity is not done with just a single yidam. There are also many kinds of deities; not just yidams, but also protectors, lamas, and so forth. The reason for so many yidams is, as they say in Tibet, "If you have thirty yaks, then you have thirty different sets of horns" which means, "If you have thirty people, you have thirty different ways of thinking." Everybody wants food, but some want bread, some want vegetables, some want rice, and so forth. In the same way, if there were only one yidam, this couldn't satisfy all the various motivations, wishes, or requirements of different people. Perhaps a particular visualization of a particular deity wouldn't be completely appropriate to bring the necessary change in everyone's mind. That is why there are so many different yidams, some peaceful, some wrathful, and so on. This was also why the Buddha with his great compassion and his incredible skill devised so many different ways to practice.

Everyone has different problems. Some have primarily the obstacle of desire, others have primarily the obstacle of anger, still others of pride or jealousy. For those with desire, there are many different categories of desire, such as attachment to possessions, attachment to fame, or to the body. Whatever the main problem, there has to be different means used to eliminate that particular problem. In general, to eliminate the problems of desire or attachment, one meditates on very peaceful, very beautiful deities. To eliminate anger, one meditates on more wrathful deities.

The idea behind meditating on a very beautiful deity, when your main problem is desire and attachment, is that you meditate on a deity which is a hundred or a thousand times more beautiful, more extraordinary than anything that you are attached to. Meditating on something that is so much more beautiful and attractive will decrease your attachment to much less beautiful things.

There is a story that shows this very clearly. The Buddha had a cousin called Gaoul and this cousin had a wife called Pundarika, who was extremely beautiful. Gaoul was very attached to her. The Buddha knew that the time had come to take his cousin onto the path of the Dharma and he wanted to persuade his cousin to become a monk. But when the Buddha came to fetch him, Gaoul's wife was extremely upset because she knew that the Buddha would make him a monk. She cried and cried and made him promise that he would come back. Then Gaoul went away with the Buddha, but all the time he kept thinking of her, remembering her, carrying a mental picture of his wife with him all the time. The Buddha kept saying that he must become a monk and there was no point clinging to samsara, but Gaoul kept thinking of his wife. Then the Buddha took him to a thick forest, and in the forest he showed him a she-monkey and asked Gaoul, "Who is more beautiful, your wife or the she-monkey?" and Gaoul replied, "Oh, there's no comparison. My wife is a thousand times more beautiful than that she-monkey." Then the Buddha through his miraculous powers took Gaoul to the paradises, and there they saw the most beautiful goddesses. Then the Buddha asked Gaul, "Who is more beautiful, your Pundarika or these goddesses?" As soon as Gaoul saw this, his attachment for his wife dissolved, because the object of his attachment had been defeated by something much more beautiful. This is the idea behind the meditation on a peaceful and beautiful yidam. In the case of anger, if one is very, very angry, then meditation on a very wrathful form will help one to gradually reduce the anger.

During visualization, we also imagine the environment as being different. We visualize where we are as transformed into a pure land or a palace of the deities. The visualization oneself as the yidam is to help us to overcome our involvement with our own body. The visualization of the environment as being very pure helps us to reduce all forms of negativity and to increase the positive aspects of mind like devotion and the appreciation of purity and so forth. Through the combination of these techniques of visualizing the outer environment as being pure and our form as being the deity, we come closer and closer to insight of the true nature of things. This subject is much more complex, but I have given a brief explanation of the visualization of an outer mandala and the deities inside it in yidam practice.

Questions

Question: If a disciple sees his master as the yidam, what does it mean? For example, some disciples of Marpa saw Marpa as a deity.

Rinpoche: This kind of experience is what one could call a pure vision. It's a form of experience that is due to exceedingly strong faith and devotion, but it isn't actually seeing the very expression of the true nature of mind. It is something that appears due to one's very strong faith and devotion. For example, if you have much faith and devotion in your guru and in the yidam, then it is possible that you will see the yidam manifesting in the form of the guru or the guru manifesting in the form of the yidam. It actually appears to you very clearly in a vision.

Question: It is said that in the *bardo* everyone has a mental form. What is this mental form and how does this mental form relate to the yidam? If one doesn't reach Buddhahood in one lifetime, does it mean that one determines one's rebirth such as being reborn in Tibet according to how much one accomplishes in yidam practice?

Rinpoche: In this life there is no mental body while we are within our ordinary samsaric existence. We only have a coarse physical body and we don't have a mental body. The mental body only appears in the bardo. This is the time when we have left behind the physical body of this life, and we have not gotten another physical body yet. So in between we have a mental form and in the bardo we have different experiences than we have with a physical body. While in a mental form, we can see the manifestation of the deities that are part of the true nature of our mind. They appear to manifest outside of us during the bardo, but this is different from what we are talking about now.

What we are speaking about now is that by using the symbolic yidam, which is a pure symbol, we can gradually bring our mind back to its purity, and finally come to the point where the symbolic yidam and real yidam unite, like the meeting of two very old friends. This is when the nature of our mind really manifests.

When we meditate on the yidam, we are not meditating on Tibet, we're meditating on a deity. The effect will not necessary make us be born in Tibet, but whatever qualities we have managed to develop through that meditation, like faith or devotion or compassion or intelligence, will, of course, remain with us and be part of us in our next lifetime.

The Middle-way Meditation Instructions

Notes

By
Clark Johnson, Ph. D.

1. Buddhists believe that the outer world that we experience such as trees and rocks are just appearances that appear to the mind. A modern example of this is water. Its form changes, appearing hard and cold (as in ice), as a liquid and flowing (as in water), or it appears as vapor and hot (as in steam). Yet its true nature is more like two Hydrogen atoms attached to one Oxygen atom.

2. The Buddhist teachings can be divided into three presentations or "turnings of the wheel of Dharma." The first is the hinayana. At this level we examine the mind carefully with shamatha and vipashyana meditation. We develop the understanding of the emptiness of person. In the second turning, the Buddha introduced the teachings on the Middle-way which were the teachings on the emptiness of phenomena as well. This turning encompasses bodhisattva activity, which involves compassion, and the desire to help all other beings (bodhichitta). The third turning involves the teachings of Buddha-nature—the essence in all beings which allows them to achieve enlightenment—and luminosity which is the potential of phenomena to manifest. This is described in greater detail in Thrangu Rinpoche's *The Three Vehicles of Buddhist Practice*.

3. We choose to use the word "empty" rather than "void" for the Sanskrit *shunyata* because *shunyata* implies "empty of inherent nature" and contains luminosity (Tib. *salwa*) out of which things manifest. Voidness implies a complete emptiness without any luminosity.

4. The practice of transference of consciousness described in this story is still taught in Tibet.

5. There are six realms and should be taken quite literally. Thrangu Rinpoche has said that in earlier times great bodhisattvas would travel to these realms and come back and tell people about them. For more detail on these realms see the chart on page ten.

6. Usually in the West meditation refers to shamatha meditation where one sits on the cushion and follows the breath. Meditation broader than this would be an analytical meditation. We would again sit shamatha until our mind was settled and then we would begin to analyze the topic one-pointedly.

7. Actually, in Eastern cultures the mind is thought to reside in the heart, not the brain. This was also believed to be true by the ancient Greeks and as a result many words for mental activities have "heart" in them which we still preserve for referring to emotions. For example, we talk about something "heartfelt" or "he broke my heart," or "not having a heart" to refer to emotions.

8. The English for this term might be "transcendental compassion" meaning compassion not just for a few persons, but for all sentient beings. In the Sanskrit bodhichitta, *bodhi* means "awakened" or "enlightened" and *chitta* means "mind," so bodhichitta means "awakened mind." Many translators prefer "awakened" over "enlightened" because the word enlightened is a non-Buddhist term that was first used when Buddhism was introduced. In Tibetan this "awakened mind" was translated as *chang chup kyi sem* in which *chang chup* means "awakened" and *kyi* is a conjunction and *sem* is "mind." So the Tibetan translators translated the Sanskrit quite literally into Tibetan.

9. Just as there are many words for cars in the United States, there are many names for mind and intelligence in Tibetan. Prajna is a Sanskrit word meaning "highest intelligence." It is close to the word "jnana" which is the intelligence of an enlightened being in contrast to the knowledge of an ordinary person. Here we are talking about a "higher knowledge" in contrast to "ordinary knowledge" such as knowledge of how a car works. Even though both are prajna. In Tibetan *prajna* was translated as *sherab* in which the first syllable *she* means mind and *rab* means "highest" or "superior."

10. This looking directly at mind is a vajrayana technique that in the Kagyu lineage came from Saraha and Naropa. This technique is called mahamudra in the Kagyu lineage and is very similar to dzogchen meditation of the Nyingma lineage. This is much more comprehensively described in Thrangu Rinpoche's *Moonbeams of Mahamudra*. Namo Buddha Publications, 2000.

11. At the Nalanda Institute of Higher Education at Rumtek monastery, the seat of His Holiness the Sixteenth Karmapa, this analytical meditation was done by having the students in the shedra (monastic college) face the outer walls of the meditation room and go into a deep meditative state. Khenpo Tsultrim Rinpoche would then read certain passages aloud, for them to contemplate.

12. Blessings are the result of many great practitioners concentrating their mental energy on the lineage or deities and as a result these develop a kind of power to help practitioners. But one must open oneself up to receive these blessings, the blessings are received if the practitioner is receptive.

13. The most common practice in a Tibetan monastery is the sadhana or "puja" in which one visualizes a deity such as Avalokiteshvara, Padmasambhava, Vajrayogini, or Tara and then at the end dissolves the deity. Thrangu Rinpoche has said that trying to keep the visualization completely in one's mind and being one-pointed in the practice is almost identical to trying to follow the breath in shamatha practice, but obviously more complicated.

14. There are several hundred monastic vows and one takes them for a lifetime. Lay persons can take the first seven for special events or practices and can vow to keep them for a day, a week, a few months, or a lifetime. The seven basic vows are: (1) not taking life, (2) not taking what is not given, (3) avoiding sexual misconduct, (4) not deceiving or lying, (5) not slandering a person, (6) avoiding harsh words, (7) avoiding empty or useless speech.

15. These seven aspects (Skt. *saptadharma-vairocana*) are: (1) a straight body and spine, (2) looking downward beyond the tip of the nose, (3) straight shoulder blades, (4) keeping the lips touching gently, (5) having the tip of the tongue touch the tip of the palate, (6) legs folded in either full or half lotus position, and (7) placing the right hand on the left hand in an egg shape with the thumbs gently touching.

16. These techniques of using a support and no support are more extensively described in Thrangu Rinpoche's *The Meditation of Mahamudra, Part I*. Boulder: Namo Buddha Publications.

17. This is Tilopa's famous six-pointed saying on meditation which goes:

"Don't reflect"	(on the past)
"Don't think"	(on the present)
"Don't anticipate"	(on the future)
"Don't meditate"	(don't treat meditation as a goal)
"Don't analyze"	(your experiences)
"Rest naturally."	(This is what you should do.)

18. This natural state is known as ordinary mind (Tib. *thamel gyi shepa*) and refers to the mind as it was before it was clouded or covered up with disturbing emotions. It is called "ordinary" not because it is like the mind that we ordinarily identify, but rather that the mind has always been this way and returning to its true nature is nothing extraordinary.

19. Thrangu Rinpoche usually begins his teachings with encouragement to raise bodhichitta and we include only this particular one to show how one applies this Middle-way technique to receiving a dharma teaching.

20. The mind is said to be empty rather than void. A "dead emptiness" like that found in a corpse does not describe the mind which has the additional quality of luminosity or intelligence.

21. When one says "analyzing," this implies a cognitive process or deduction similar to what we do in ordinary life when we analyze a problem. When one says "looking," this implies that one receives the problem directly without doing any cognitive or discursive activities.

22. By this we mean that the feeling has an appearance because we can obviously feel and describe it, but it does not have an inherent existence because we can never find it and point to it and say "there it is" as we can with a solid object.

23. On the relative level pinching the skin of the person will cause pain. This is the interdependence and at this level no one will deny that pain is felt. In other teachings Rinpoche has said that the technique of pinching was actually used in Tibetan monasteries to illustrate this concept.

24. In the Madhyamaka (Middle-way) there are eight conscious-nesses. First are the five sensory consciousnesses of eye, ear, tongue, nose, and body and the mental consciousness in which

all the thoughts and feelings appear. These are well described in the hinayana as well as the mahayana. But in the mahayana there is also the seventh afflicted or klesha consciousness, which is always present and is essentially the feeling of "I" and "mine." Then there is the eighth consciousness, called the storehouse or alaya consciousness, which stores all the thoughts and feelings as well as their karmic impressions. When we are asleep and dream, for example, the sensory consciousnesses are turned off and so our dream material comes from the eighth consciousness. Since we don't know better, we mistake these impressions for reality and hence believe what is happening while we are dreaming is real. This is described in greater detail in Thrangu Rinpoche's *Differentiating Consciousness and Wisdom.*

25. The Tibetan word for "meditation" is *sgom* which is very close to the Tibetan word for "habituation" or "getting used to," which is *goms*. These words have the same root.

26. This is explained in Thrangu Rinpoche's *Moonbeams of Mahamudra* Boulder: Namo Buddha Publications, 2000.

27. Deities of Hinduism and other religions are different from Buddhist deities in that Buddhists recognize that the deities are created by mind.

A Brief Biography of Thrangu Rinpoche

Thrangu Rinpoche was born in Kham in 1933. At the age of five he was formally recognized by the Sixteenth Karmapa and the previous Situ Rinpoche as the incarnation of the great Thrangu tulku. Entering Thrangu monastery, from the ages of seven to sixteen he studied reading, writing, grammar, poetry, and astrology, memorized ritual texts, and completed two preliminary retreats. At sixteen under the direction of Khenpo Lodro Rabsel he began the study of the three vehicles of Buddhism while staying in retreat.

At twenty-three he received full ordination from the Karmapa. When he was 26, Rinpoche left Tibet for India at the time of the Chinese military takeover. He was called to Rumtek, Sikkim, where the Karmapa had his seat in exile. At 35 he took the geshe examination before 1500 monks at Buxador monastic refugee camp in Bengal, and was awarded the degree of Geshe Lharampa. On his return to Rumtek he was named Abbot of Rumtek monastery and the Nalanda Institute for Higher Buddhist studies. He has been the personal teacher of the four principal Karma Kagyu tulkus: Shamar Rinpoche, Situ Rinpoche, Jamgon Kongtrul Rinpoche and Gyaltsab Rinpoche.

Thrangu Rinpoche has traveled extensively throughout Europe, the Far East and North America. In 1984 he spent several months in Tibet where he ordained over 100 monks and nuns and visited several monasteries. In Nepal he has built a monastery in Boudhanath, a retreat center and college at Namo Buddha, an abbey for nuns in Kathmandu, and a school in Boudhanath for the general education of lay children and young monks.

In October of 1999 he consecrate the College at Sarnath which will accept students from the different sects of Buddhism and will be available to western students as well.

Thrangu Rinpoche has given teachings for over 20 years in over 25 countries and is especially known for taking complex teachings and making them accessible to Western students. Just recently when his Holiness the 17th Karmapa fled from Tibet, the Dalai Lama appointed Thrangu Rinpoche to be his tutor.

The Glossary

Abhidharma (Tib. *chö ngön pa*) The Buddhist teachings are often divided into the Tripitaka: the Sutras (teachings of the Buddha), the Vinaya (teachings on conduct), and the Abhidharma which are the analyses of phenomena that exist primarily as a commentarial addition to the Buddhist teachings. There is not, in fact, an Abhidharma section within the Tibetan collection of the Buddhist teachings.

alaya consciousness (Tib. *kün shi nam she*) According to the Yogacara school this is the eighth consciousness and is often called the ground consciousness or store-house consciousness.

arhat (Tib. *dra chom pa*) Accomplished hinayana practitioners who have eliminated the klesha obscurations. They are the fully realized Shravakas and Pratyekabuddhas.

Avalokiteshvara (Tib. *Chenrezig*) Deity of compassion. Known as the patron deity of Tibet, his mantra is OM MANI PADME HUM.

bardo (Tib.) Literally, bardo means "between the two." There are six kinds of bardos, but here it refers to the time between death and a rebirth in a new body.

blessings (Skt. *adhishthana*, Tib. *chin lap*) When a student has true devotion, she becomes receptive and can receive inspiration from external sources such as deities or great practitioners. This inspiration is called blessings or splendor waves.

bodhichitta (Tib. *chang chup chi sem*) Literally, the mind of enlightenment. There are two kinds of bodhichitta: absolute bodhichitta, which is completely awakened mind that sees the emptiness of phenomena, and relative bodhichitta which is the aspiration to practice the six paramitas and free all beings from the suffering of samsara.

bodhisattva (Tib. *chang chup sem pa*) Literally, one who exhibits the mind of enlightenment. Also an individual who has committed him or herself to the mahayana path of compassion and the practice of the six paramitas to achieve Buddhahood to free all beings from samsara.

bodhisattva levels (Skt. *bhumi*, Tib. *sa*) The levels or stages a bodhisattva goes through to reach enlightenment. These consist of ten levels in the sutra tradition and thirteen in the tantra tradition.

brahmin A Hindu of the highest caste who usually performs priestly functions.

Buddha-nature (Skt. *tathagatagarbha*, Tib. *de shin shek pay nying po*) The original nature present in all beings which when realized leads to enlightenment. It is often called the essence of Buddhahood or enlightened essence.

Chenresig (Skt. *Avalokiteshvara*) Deity of compassion.

chod practice (Tib.) Pronounced "chö." This literally means "to cut off" and refers to a practice that is designed to cut off all ego involvement and defilements. The *mo chod* (female chod) practice was founded by the famous female saint Machig Labdron (1031 to 1129 C.E.).

clarity (Tib. *salwa*) Also called luminosity. In the vajrayana everything is void, but this voidness is not completely empty because it has clarity. Clarity allows all phenomena to appear in emptiness and is a characteristic of emptiness (Skt. *shunyata*).

conditioned existence See samsara.

consciousnesses, eight (Skt. *vijnana*, Tib. *nam she tsog gye*) These are the five sensory consciousnesses of sight, hearing, smell, taste, touch, and body sensation. Sixth is mental consciousness, seventh is afflicted consciousness, and eighth is ground consciousness.

creation stage (Skt. *utpattikrama*, Tib. *che rim*) In the vajrayana there are two stages of meditation: the creation or development stage and the completion stage. This is a method of tantric meditation that involves visualization and contemplation on deities for the purpose of realizing the purity of all phenomena. In this creation stage visualization of the deity is established and maintained.

cyclic existence (Skt. *samsara*, Tib. *khor wa*) Ordinary existence, which contains suffering because one still possesses attachment, aggression, and ignorance. It is contrasted to liberation or nirvana.

dharma (Tib. *chö*) This has two main meanings: Any truth such as the sky is blue and secondly, as used in this text, the teachings of the Buddha (also called Buddhadharma).

dharmakaya (Tib. *chö ku*) One of the three bodies of Buddhahood. It is enlightenment itself, that is wisdom beyond reference point. See kayas, three.

emptiness (Skt. *Shunyata* Tib. *tong pa nyi*) Also translated as voidness. The Buddha taught in the second turning of the wheel of dharma that external phenomena and internal phenomena, including the concept of self or "I," have no real existence and therefore are "empty."

Gampopa (1079-1153 C.E.) One of the main lineage holders of the Kagyu lineage in Tibet. Known also for writing the *Jewel Ornament of Liberation*.

geshe (Tib.) A scholar who has attained a doctorate in Buddhist studies. This usually takes fifteen to twenty years to attain.

ground consciousness See consciousnesses, eight

Hashang Mahayana A master of Chinese Buddhism who advocated the rapid path to enlightenment. He was defeated in debate by Kamalashila at Samye monastery and as a result, left Tibet. The gradual path of meditation consequently was taught in Tibet.

hinayana (Tib. *tek pa chung wa*) The term refers to the first set of teachings of the Buddha that emphasized the careful examination of mind and compassion. This path is very important to the modern Theravada Buddhists.

insight meditation (Skt. *vipashyana*, Tib. *lhak thong*) Meditation that develops insight into the nature of mind. The other main meditation is Shamatha meditation.

interdependent origination Skt. *pratityasamutpada*, Tib. *ten drel)* The twelve successive phases that begin with ignorance and end with old age and death.

jnana (Tib. *yeshe*) Enlightened wisdom which is beyond dualistic thought.

Kagyu (Tib.) One of the four major schools of Buddhism in Tibet. It was founded by Marpa and is headed by His Holiness Karmapa. The other three are the Nyingma, the Sakya, and the Gelukpa schools.

Kamalashila An eighth century scholar in India who was a student of Shantarakshita and is best known for coming to Tibet and debating and defeating the Chinese scholar Hashang Mahayana at Samye monastery and then writing the *Stages of Meditation*.

khenpo (Tib.) A title of someone who has completed many years of study of Buddhism. It can also mean an abbot of a monastery.

kayas, three (Tib. *ku sum*) There are three bodies of the Buddha: the nirmanakaya, sambhogakaya and dharmakaya. The dharmakaya, also called the "truth body," is the complete enlightenment or the complete wisdom of the Buddha which is unoriginated wisdom beyond form. The buddhas manifest in the sambhogakaya and the nirmanakaya. The sambhogakaya, also called the "enjoyment body," manifests only to bodhisattvas. The nirmanakaya, also called the "emanation body," manifests in the world and in this context manifests as Shakyamuni Buddha.

Madhyamaka (Tib. *u ma*) This is a philosophical school founded by Nagarjuna in the second century. The main principle of this school is proving that everything is empty of self-nature as usually understood, using rational reasoning.

mahamudra (Tib. *cha ja chen po*) Literally means "great seal" or "great symbol." This meditative transmission emphasizes the understanding of phenomena as they truly are, by using techniques that look at mind directly to see the emptiness of self and phenomena.

mahasiddha (Tib. *drup thop chen po*) A practitioner who has a great deal of realization.

mandala (Tib. *chin kor*) A meditative diagram used in various vajrayana practices which usually has a central deity and four directions or gates.

Marpa (1012-1097 C.E.) Marpa was a Tibetan who made three trips to India and brought back many tantric texts including the Six Yogas of Naropa, the Guhyasamaja, and the Chakrasamvara practices. His teacher was Tilopa and he founded the Kagyu lineage in Tibet.

Middle-way (Tib. *u ma*) or Madhyamaka School. A philosophical school founded by Nagarjuna and based on the Prajnaparamita sutras of emptiness.

Milarepa (1040-1123 C.E.) Milarepa was a student of Marpa who attained enlightenment in one lifetime. His student Gampopa founded the (Dagpo) Kagyu lineage.

Nagarjuna (Tib. *ludrup)* An Indian scholar of the second century who founded the Madhyamaka philosophical school which emphasized emptiness.

Naropa (956-1040 C.E.) An Indian master best known for transmitting many vajrayana teachings to Marpa, who took them back to Tibet before they became mostly lost in India.

nirmanakaya (Tib. *tulku)* There are three bodies of the Buddha; the nirmanakaya or "emanation body" manifests in the world and in this context manifests as Shakyamuni Buddha. See kayas, three.

Padmasambhava (Tib. *Guru Rinpoche*) He was invited to Tibet in the ninth century C.E. and is known for pacifying the non-Buddhist forces and founding the Nyingma lineage.

pandita (Tib. *pandita)* A great scholar.

paramitas, six (Tib. *parol tu chinpa)* Sanskrit for "perfections;" the Tibetan literally means "gone to the other side." These are the six practices of the mahayana path: transcendent generosity (Skt. *dana*), transcendent discipline (Skt. *shila*), transcendent patience (Skt. *kshanti*), transcendent exertion (Skt. *virya*), transcendent meditation (Skt. *dhyana*), and transcendent knowledge (Skt. *prajna*). The ten paramitas are these plus aspirational prayer, power, and prajna.

phowa (Tib.) An advanced tantric practice concerned with the ejection of consciousness at death to a favorable realm.

prajna (Tib. *she rab)* In Sanskrit it means "perfect knowledge" and can mean wisdom, understanding, or discrimination. Usually it means the wisdom of seeing things from a high (e.g. non-dualistic) point of view.

rinpoche Literally, "very precious," used as a term of respect for a Tibetan guru.

shamatha or tranquility meditation (Tib. *shine)* Basic sitting meditation in which one usually follows the breath while observing the workings of the mind while sitting in the cross-legged posture.

sambhogakaya (Tib. *long chö dzok ku)* There are three bodies of the Buddha and the sambhogakaya, also called the "enjoyment body," is a form of the dharmakaya which only manifests to bodhisattvas. See the three kayas.

samsara (Tib. *kor wa*) Conditioned existence of ordinary life in which suffering occurs because one still possesses attachment, aggression, and ignorance. It is contrasted to nirvana.

Samye temple The first monastery built in Tibet in 750-770 C.E.

Shantarakshita (8th century C.E.) An abbot of Nalanda University who was invited by King Trisong Detsen to come to Tibet. He established Samye Monastery and thus helped introduce Buddhism to Tibet.

Shantideva (675 to 725 C.E.) A great bodhisattva who lived in India, known for his two works on the conduct of a bodhisattva, particular his *Guide to a Bodhisattva's Way of Life*.

Saraha One of the eighty-four mahasiddhas of India who was known for his spiritual songs about mahamudra.

shastra (Tib. *tan chö*) The Buddhist teachings are divided into the words of the Buddha (the sutras) and the commentaries of others on his words (the shastras).

sending and taking practice (Tib. *tong len*) A meditation practice promulgated by Atisha in which the practitioner takes in the negative conditions of others and gives out all that is positive.

six realms of samsara (Tib. *rikdruk*) These are the possible types of rebirths for beings in samsara and are: the god realm in which gods have great pride, the asura realm in which the jealous gods try to maintain what they have, the human realm which is the best realm because one has the possibility of achieving enlightenment, the animal realm characterized by stupidity, the hungry ghost realm characterized by great craving, and the hell realm characterized by aggression.

Shravaka (Tib. *nyen thö*) Literally "those who hear," meaning disciples. A type of realized hinayana practitioner (arhat) who has achieved the realization of the nonexistence of a personal self.

shunyata (Tib. *tong pa nyi*) Usually translated as voidness or emptiness. The Buddha taught in the second turning of the wheel of dharma that external phenomena and internal phenomena including the concept of self or "I" have no real existence and therefore are "empty."

sutra (Tib. *do*) These are the hinayana and mahayana texts which are the words of the Buddha. These are often contrasted with the tantras, which are the Buddha's vajrayana teachings, and the shastras, which are commentaries on the words of the Buddha.

tantra (Tib. *gyu*) The texts of the vajrayana practices.

Tara (Tib. *drolma*) A female meditation deity, often called the mother of all Buddhas. Also considered the patron saint of Tibet. Tara is common to all four lineages. Green Tara is associated with protection while White Tara is associated with healing and long life.

thangka (Tib.) A Tibetan religious scroll.

Theravada (Skt. *Sthavsravada*, Tib. *neten depa*) Specifically a school of the hinayana. Here refers to the first teachings of the Buddha, which emphasized the careful examination of mind and its confusion.

Tripitaka (Tib. *de nö sum*) Literally, the three baskets. There are the sutras (the narrative teachings of the Buddha), the Vinaya (a code for monks and nuns) and the Abhidharma (philosophical background of the dharma).

Trisong Detsen (790 to 858 C.E.) A king of Tibet who invited great Indian saints and yogis to Tibet to propagate the dharma. He also directed the construction of Tibet's first monastery (Samye Ling).

Tilopa (928-1009 C.E.) One of the 84 mahasiddhas who became the guru of Naropa who transmitted his teachings to the Kagyu lineage in Tibet.

tranquillity meditation See shamatha.

Vairocana (Tib. *nam par nang dze*) The sambhogakaya buddha of the buddha family.

vajra (Tib. *dorje*) Usually translated "diamond like." This may be an implement held in the hand during certain vajrayana ceremonies, or it can refer to a quality that is so pure and so enduring that it is like a diamond.

vajrayana (Tib. *dorje tek pa*) There are three major traditions of Buddhism (hinayana, mahayana, and vajrayana). The vajrayana is based on the tantras, emphasizes the clarity aspect of phenomena, and is mainly practiced in Tibet.

Vajrayogini (Tib. *Dorje Palmo*) A female meditational deity belonging to the anuttarayogatantra who is often red in color and dancing with a semi-wrathful facial expression.

vipashyana meditation (Tib. *lha tong*) Sanskrit for "insight meditation." This meditation develops insight into the nature of mind. The other main meditation is shamatha meditation.

yidam (Tib.) A tantric deity that embodies qualities of Buddhahood and is the basis for practice in the vajrayana.

Glossary of Tibetan Terms

bardo	bar do	intermediate
cha ja chen po	phyag rgya chen po	mahamudra
chang chup chi sem	byang chub kyi sems	bodhichitta
che rim	bskyed rim	develop. stage
Chenrezig	spyan ras gzigs	Avalokiteshvara
chin kor	dkyil 'khor	mandala
chö	chos	dharma
chod	gcod	cutting practice
chö chi ku	chos kyi sku	dharmakaya
de nö sum	sde snod gsum	Tripitaka
de shin shek pay nying po	de bzhin gshegs pa'i nying po	Buddha-nature
do	mdo	sutra
dorje	rdo rje	vajra
dra chom pa	dgra bcom pa	arhat
drup thop chen po	grub thob chen po	mahasiddha
geshe	dge bshes	high scholar
guru rinpoche	gu ru rin po che	Padmasambhava
gyu	rgyud	tantra
lhagthong	lhag mthong	vipashyana
kagyu	bka' brgyud	Kagyu lineage
khenpo	mkhan po	abbot
khor wa	'khor ba	samsara
ku sum	sku gsum	three kayas
kun shi nam she	kun gzhi' rnam shes	alaya consciousness
long cho dzok ku	long spyod rdzogs sku	sambhogakaya
mo cho	mo chod	mother chod
nam par nang dze	rnam par snag mdzad	Vairocana
nam she tsog gye	rnam shes	conscious., eight
neten dapa	gnas brtan pa' sde	Theravadin
nyen thö	nyan thos	Shravaka
nyinje	sning rje	compassion
parol tu chinpa	phar phyin	paramitas, six
phowa	'pho ba	transfer conscious.
rikdruk	rigs drug gi skye gnas	6 realms of samsara
sa	sa	bodhisattva levels
salwa	gsal ba	luminosity
she rab	shes rab	prajna
shine	zhi gnas	shamatha

tan chö	bstan bcos	shastra
tek pa chung wa	theg pa chung ba	hinayana
ten drel	rten 'brel	dependent origin.
thangka	than ka	scroll painting
tong len	gtong len	sending and taking
tong pa nyi	strong pa nyid	emptiness
tulku	sprul sku	incarnation
u ma	dbu ma	Madhyamaka
yeshe	ye shes	wisdom
yidam	yi dam	meditation deity

The Bibliography

The Sutras

The Heart Sutra A sutra by the Buddha which is a condensation of the Prajnaparamita teachings on emptiness. This sutra is chanted daily in most mahayana centers.

Others

Asanga and Maitreya *The Uttara Tantra.* (Skt. *Mahayana-sutra-uttara-shastra*, Tib. *theg pa chen po rgyud bla ma' i bstan bcos*, Pron. *"gyu lama"*)
Published by Namo Buddha Publications with a translation of the 404 root verses and a commentary by Thrangu Rinpoche.

Gampopa *Jewel Ornament of Liberation.* (Tib. *thar pa rgyan*)
Originally translated by Herbert Guenther in a very difficult translation. Also translated by Ken and Katia Holmes as *Jewels of Dharma: Jewels of Freedom* in a very loose translation. The reader should see the excellent translation by Konchog Gyaltsen Rinpoche called *The Jewel Ornament of Liberation.* Ithaca: Snow Lion, 1998.

Kamalashila *The Stages of Meditation.* (Skt. *bhavanakrama*, Tib. *sgom pa'i rim pa,* Pron. *gom rim*).
This text is in three volumes and was written by Kamalashila (8th century C.E.) and laid the foundation for teaching the gradual path in Tibetan Buddhism. *The Stages of Meditation* have been translated into English by Parmananda Sharma as the *Bhavanakrama of Kamalishila.* Ithaca: Snow Lion Publishing, 1998. A commentary on this volume by Thrangu Rinpoche will be available in 2000 from Namo Buddha Publications.

Mipham Rinpoche *The Gateway to Knowledge.* (Tib. *mkhas pa'i tshul la jug pa'i sgo zhes bya ba'i bstan bcos bzhugs so*).
This is an encyclopedia of knowledge. The first volume has been translated by Erik Pema Kusang (Hong Kong: Rangjung Yeshe Books, 1997).

Rangjung Dorje (the Third Karmapa) *Differentiating Consciousness and Wisdom.* (Tib. *rnam shes ye shes 'byed pa*, Pron. *namshe yeshe gepa*)
This is a text in Buddhist psychology and was written to describe the eight consciousnesses and how they are transformed into the five

wisdoms upon attaining enlightenment. The text and a commentary is available from Namo Buddha Publications.

Shantideva *A Guide to the Bodhisattva's Way of Life* (Skt. *Bodh-icaryavatara*, Tib. *byang chub sems dpa'i spyod pa la 'jug pa*)
Translated by Steven Batchelor as *A Guide to the Bodhisattva's Way of Life* Dharmasala: Archives of Tibetan Works. Also a translation of the root text and a commentary by Thrangu Rinpoche is available as *The Guide to a Bodhisattva's Way of Life*. Boulder: Namo Buddha Publications.

Thrangu Rinpoche *Three Vehicles of Buddhist Practice.* Boulder: Namo Buddha Publications, 1998.

This book gives an outline of the three vehicles.

Thrangu Rinpoche *The Tibetan Vinaya: A Guide to Buddhist Conduct.* Boulder: Namo Buddha Publications, 1995.

This text gives an explanation of the three vows (Tib. *dum gsum*) of the hinayana, mahayana, and vajrayana and tells how Buddhists should conduct themselves.

Thrangu Rinpoche *Moonbeams of Mahamudra* To be published by Namo Buddha Publications in 2000.

This is an overview of mahamudra, the principal meditation of the Kagyu lineage. This overview is based on Tashi Namgyal's *Mahamudra: The Quintessence of Mind.*

Thrangu Rinpoche *The Practice of Tranquillity and Insight.* Snow Lion Publications, 1998.

A detailed look at shamatha and vipashyana and their union. The book is based on the seventh chapter of Jamgon Kongtrul's eighth chapter of the *Treasury of Knowledge.*

Thrangu Rinpoche *The Open Door to Emptiness.* Vancouver: Karme Thekchen Choling.

A detailed commentary on the logical arguments used in establishing that all persons and phenomena are empty of inherent nature. In this book based on Mipham Rinpoche's encyclopedic work Thrangu Rinpoche gives a non-technical explanation of the arguments for emptiness.

Thrangu Rinpoche *A Guide to Shamatha Meditation.* Boulder: Namo Buddha Publications, 1995.

This is a booklet based on Pema Karpo's *Meditation Instructions* that summarizes shamatha and vipashyana meditation from the mahamudra perspective.

A *Guide to the Bodhisattva's Way of Life*, 62
agitation, 55
analytical meditation, 37, 50
anger, 20, 75, 84, 103
arhats, 19
attachment, 22
bardo, 104
blessing, 102
bliss, 88
bodhichitta, 11, 19, 25, 27, 45, 70, 75, 99
bodhisattva levels, 35
bodhisattvas, 11, 19
Brahmin, 82, 86
Buddha, 35, 61
Buddha-nature, 99, 101
causes of things, 39
Chenrezig, 100, 102
chod, 8
Christian, 42, 44
clarity, 88
cognitive obscurations, 21
commentaries (Skt. *shastra*), 36
compassion, 11, 16, 23, 25, 45, 97, 99
conditioned existence, 53
creation stage, 100
creator, 41
cultivation, 88
cutting thoughts, 70-73
Dampa Sangye, 8
desire, 103
devotion, 96
Dharma, 5, 76

dharmakaya, 43
direct examination of mind, 50-51
direct looking, 84
emotional obscurations, 21
emptiness, 93
empty, 84
forgetfulness, 54
Gampopa, 79, 90
Gaoul, 103
gathering virtue, 51-52
genuine compassion, 28
gods, 99
ground consciousness, 85
guru yoga meditation, 51
happiness, 69
Hashang Mahayana, 6
healing nectar, 18, 25
Heart Sutra, 40
hinayana, 23, 28
Hindu religion, 99
illusion to be our present reality, 85
insight meditation, 63
instantaneously path, 7
Kagyu lineage, 90
Kamalashila, 5, 11, 91
karmic obscurations, 21
laziness, 53
listening to the teachings, 34-36
looking directly, 83
luminosity, 93
mahasiddha, 8
Marpa, 58, 90, 104
meditation, 88

Other Paperback Books by Thrangu Rinpoche

The Three Vehicles of Buddhist Practice. This book gives an overview of the Hinayana, Mahayana, and Vajrayana as it was practiced in Tibet. Boulder: Namo Buddha Publications, 1998.

The Open Door to Emptiness. This book goes through in a easy-to-understand way the arguments made to establish that all phenomena are indeed empty. Vancouver: Karme Thekchen Choling, 1997.

The Practice of Tranquillity and Insight. This book is a practical guide to the two types of meditation that form the core of Buddhist spiritual practice. Ithaca: Snow Lion Publications, 1993

Buddha Nature. This book is an overview of the whole concept of Buddha-nature as it is presented in Maitreya's *Uttara Tantra.* Kathamandu: Rangjung Yeshe Publications, 1993.

The King of Samadhi. This book is a commentary on the only sutra of the Buddha which discusses mahamudra meditation. It is also the sutra which predicted the coming of Gampopa. Kathmandu: Rangjung Yeshe Publications, 1994.

The Songs of Naropa. This book tells the story of the life of Naropa and analyzes in detail his famous Summary of Mahamudra which lays out the path of mahamudra meditation by the guru whose succession of students went on to found the Kagyu lineage. Kathmandu: Rangjung Yeshe Publications, 1997.